DIVERTICULITIS COOKBOOK

*A Complete Diet Guide for People with Diverticulitis.
High Fiber Breakfast, Main Courses, Soup, Snacks &
Liquid and Low Residue Diet*

BARBARA CAMERON

CONTENTS

BREAKFAST RECIPES

MAIN DISHES RECIPES

SOUP RECIPES

SALAD RECIPES

SNACK RECIPES

HOLIDAY RECIPES

Introduction

Although the terms may sound familiar, treatment options for diverticulosis and diverticulitis are quite different. For example, treatment for diverticulitis may involve surgery, or antibiotics followed with clear liquid or low residue diets, while treatment for diverticulosis usually may only involve dietary modifications towards a greater consumption of fiber. Both conditions are typically prevalent in the Western world, since studies show that fiber consumption is not high.

The recipes and supplemental information contained in this guide are here to empower you with the information you need to increase the fiber in your diet, thus lessening your chances of developing diverticulosis or preventing the occurrence of diverticulitis. The increase in fiber should help the passage of digested food through your intestine. It will allow more normal bowel movements and reduce abdominal pain.

We hope that the information provided in this guide will be beneficial for you as you begin your journey to a high fiber lifestyle. Please remember to discuss any new dietary options with your personal physician or dietician prior to beginning any new nutritional program.

Recipe Guidelines

DIVERTICULITIS

Clear Liquid

If the symptoms of diverticulitis are severe, a clear liquid diet is recommended. Going without solid food gives the colon a chance to rest and heal. The doctor may recommend a clear liquid diet immediately after surgery until your digestive system regains the strength to absorb and digest fiber. A clear liquid diet is typically followed by a low residue (or low fiber) diet.

Low Residue

A low-residue diet is recommended during the flare-up periods of diverticulitis. This diet aims to decrease bowel volume so that the infection can heal. An intake of less than 10 grams of fiber per day is generally considered a low residue diet. If you have been on a low-residue diet for an extended period of time, your doctor may recommend a daily multi-vitamin/mineral supplement. At the end of your low residue diet, you should slowly begin adding more high fiber foods into your diet.

. . .

DIVERTICULOSIS

High Fiber

Once the pain of diverticulitis subsides, a high fiber diet is the recommended nutritional therapy in avoiding future occurrences.

Clear Liquid Diet for Diverticulitis

The following foods are allowed in a clear liquid diet:

- Plain water
- juices without pulp, such as apple juice, grape juice or cranberry juice
- Strained lemonade or fruit punch
- Bouillon, broths, fat free consommé, and strained vegetable broth
- Clear sodas or sports drinks
- Plain gelatin
- Jelly (without seeds), honey
- Ice pops without bits of fruit or fruit pulp
- Tea or coffee with no cream

A TYPICAL MENU ON THE CLEAR LIQUID DIET MAY LOOK LIKE THIS.

BREAKFAST:

- One glass fruit juice
- One cup broth
- One bowl gelatin

Morning Snack:

- One cup coffee or tea (without cream)
- One bowl gelatin

Lunch:

- One glass fruit juice and one glass water
- One cup broth
- One bowl gelatin

Evening Snack:

- One ice pop (without fruit pulp)
- One cup coffee (without cream) or tea or soft drink

Dinner:

- One cup juice or water
- One cup broth
- One bowl gelatin
- One cup coffee or tea (without cream)

Low Residue Diet for Diverticulitis

Immediately after your liquid diet therapy, you are advised to follow a low residue or low fiber diet. A low residue diet limits the amount of dietary fiber and residue-providing food in your diet. Following a low residue diet is generally limited to one or two weeks. We recommend that you discuss your specific timeline for low residue diet with your physician.

Food Group	Foods Allowed	Foods to Avoid
Beverages	Coffee, tea, decaf coffee and tea, cocoa, carbonated beverages, fruit flavored drinks without pulp.	Any beverages containing foods not allowed; alcoholic beverages
Breads and Cereals 6-11 servings	Refined white, light wheat or rye bread and rolls; saltines, or soda crackers. All refined, cooked and ready-to-eat cereals (oats, wheat and rice) such as Malt-O-Meal, Special K, Cheerios, Post Toasties.	Rolls with nuts, seeds, coconut or fruit not allowed; bread containing cracked wheat particles or whole seeds; coarse, dry cereals; any with bran or raisins. Graham crackers, corn bread.
Desserts (Avoid too many sweets)	All plain puddings, custards, tapioca, gelatin desserts, smooth ice cream, fruit ice, plain sherbet, yogurt, cake and cookies.	Rich pastries or cakes. Those with berries, nuts, seeds, raisins, coconut, dates or fruits not allowed.
Eggs 3/week	All	Egg dishes prepared with ingredients not allowed.
Fats Use in moderation	Butter, margarine, cooking oil, cream, Milk, salad dressings and mayonnaise, as tolerated. Plain gravies.	Nuts, olives.
Fruits and Fruit Juices 2 servings a day	Fruit juice without pulp. Canned: applesauce, cherries, fruit cocktail, peaches Fresh: bananas, cherries, grapefruit, melon, nectarines, peaches, plums	Prune juice Canned: pineapple, pears Fresh: apples, apricot, avocado, berries, mango, pear, dried dates, figs, prunes, raisins
Meat or Meat	Tender, broiled, stewed roast beef, veal,	Fried: meats, fish or

substitute 5-7 ounces per day	lamb, pork, ham, bacon, poultry, fish, clams, oysters, liver, kidneys; Cream cheese, cottage, American, cheddar, Swiss or jack cheese, smooth peanut butter.	poultry; meats highly seasoned or containing whole spices; sausage, frankfurters. Strong cheeses or those containing seeds. Dried beans or peas, chunky peanut butter. All others not listed as allowed.
Milk Limit to 2 cups per day	All	None except those with seeds, nuts or fruits not allowed. For low residue, limit milk to 2 cups per day.
Soups	Creamed soups with pureed or whole allowed vegetables; strained vegetable soups or chowders, meat or fish broths.	Highly seasoned soups or those containing ingredients other than on allowed list.
Vegetables and Vegetable Juice 2 servings per day	Cooked or canned artichoke hearts, asparagus, beets, carrots, chard, green and wax beans, bean sprouts, mushrooms, potato, pumpkin. Fresh and cooked tomato (no seeds or skins), stewed, pastes, purees. Tomato juice. Limit vegetables to 2 servings/per day and less than 2 grams of fiber per serving	All other raw, strongly flavored vegetables (cabbage, broccoli, cauliflower, summer squash, okra, Brussels sprouts, parsnips, rutabagas, turnips, onions, corn, baked beans). All others not listed as allowed.

Sample Daily Low Residue Meal Plan*

Breakfast

- ½ cup fruit juice
- 1 egg
- ½ cup rice cereal with 1 cup milk
- 2 slices enriched white toast
- 2 tsp. margarine
- 2 tsp jelly
- Beverage

Lunch

- 2 slices enriched white bread
- 1 tsp. margarine or mayo
- 2 oz. meat (such as turkey or ham)
- ½ cup cooked vegetable (cooked carrots)
- 1 serving fruit or fruit dessert
- Beverage

DINNER

- 3 oz. meat (cooked chicken)
- ½ cup vegetable (potato)
- ½ cup vegetable (mushrooms)
- 1 serving enriched white bread
- 1 tsp. margarine
- 1 serving dessert (vanilla pudding)
- 1 cup low-fat milk
- Beverage

High Fiber Guidelines

From this point forward, this cookbook will focus on high fiber dietary guidelines and recipes. Eating a high fiber diet is your key to preventing future outbreaks of diverticulitis.

The United States Institute of Medicine (IOM) of the National Academy of Sciences has set dietary reference intakes (DRIs) for fiber based on research data that applies to American and Canadian populations. DRIs provide nutrition guidance to both health professionals and consumers. The current daily DRIs for fiber are as follows:

- Children ages 1-3 years: 19 grams
- Children ages 4-18 years: 25 grams
- Men ages 19-50: 38 grams
- Men age 51 and older: 30 grams
- Girls ages 9-18: 26 grams
- Adult women ages 19-50: 25 grams
- Women age 51 and older: 21 grams
- Pregnant women: 28 grams
- Breastfeeding women: 29 grams

As you begin to make your transition to a high fiber diet, please note that fiber should be increased in the diet gradually. If fiber intake increases suddenly, abdominal pain, gas, and diarrhea may result. The nutritional guidelines we follow allow for five grams or more fiber per serving. Also, it is best to increase the fiber gradually. Increasing it too quickly can cause abdominal gas and diarrhea. So, add just a few grams at a time to allow the intestinal tract to adjust. While increasing your fiber intake, be sure to increase your water consumption. As a good rule of thumb, if you are not already drinking over 6 glasses of liquid a day, drink at least 2 more glasses of water a day when you increase your fiber intake.

As a precaution, you may want to avoid eating foods that contain seeds or nuts; such as popcorn, raisins, whole-kernel corn, and peanuts. A complete list of potential foods to avoid is available in this book as well.

Foods to Avoid

Some doctors still urge caution when eating seeds and foods with seeds (berries, melons, tomatoes, etc.). The concern is that the seeds might become logged in the diverticulum and cause inflammation. Although there is no scientific evidence to prove this theory, we have omitted seeds and nuts from our recipes and encourage you to speak with your physician regarding their suitability in your diet.

Seeds & Nuts (Avoid all types)

Vegetables

Chili Peppers

- Corn
- Cucumber (only English is acceptable)
- Green Peppers (Acceptable if seeds are removed)
- Tomato (Acceptable if seeds are removed)

FRUITS

- Blackberries
- Blueberries
- Coconuts
- Whole Cranberries (Cranberry Relish)
- Figs
- Grapes with seeds
- Kiwi
- Pomegranates
- Raspberries
- Strawberries
- Watermelon (Acceptable if seedless)

BREADS/STARCHES

- Bread or rolls with nuts/seeds
- Popcorn
- Wild Rice

SWEETS

- Candy with nuts/seeds
- Jam with Seeds
- Pie/Cake with nuts/seeds Raisins with Seeds

Foods to Have on Hand

Here's a handy reference to some of the foods that you should have around your kitchen. These are mainly high fiber foods.

FRUITS/JUICES

- Apple Juice
- Apple Sauce
- Apples
- Apricots
- Bananas
- Dates
- Lemon Juice
- Lime Juice
- Mangoes
- Oranges/Juice
- Peaches
- Prunes

VEGETABLES

- Alfalfa Sprouts
- Artichoke Hearts
- Asparagus
- Avocados
- Black Olives
- Broccoli
- Butternut Squash
- Cabbage
- Carrots
- Cauliflower
- Celery
- Eggplants
- Garlic
- Green Bell Peppers (seedless)
- Green Olives
- Green Onions
- Leeks
- Mushrooms
- Lettuce
- Olives
- Onions
- Peas (frozen, cooked)
- Pimento
- Red Bell Peppers (seedless)
- Russet Potatoes
- Shallots
- Spinach
- Sugar Snap Peas
- Summer Squash
- Yellow Peppers (seedless)
- Tomatoes (seedless)
- Water chestnuts
- Yams
- Zucchini

BEANS/LEGUMES

- Black Beans
- Butter Beans
- Cannellini Beans
- Garbanzo Beans
- Kidney Beans (can)
- Lentils
- Lima Beans (can)
- Navy Beans (can)
- Red Beans (can)

BREADS/STARCHES

- All Bran Cereal
- Barley
- Brown Rice
- Fiber One Cereal
- Long Grain Rice
- Oat Bran
- Rolled Oats
- Whole Wheat Tortellini
- Whole Wheat Flour
- Whole Wheat Pasta
- Whole Wheat Pita
- Whole Wheat Tortillas
- Whole Wheat Bread

MEATS

- Crab Meat, Cooked
- Ground Beef, Lean
- Ground Turkey, Lean
- Lean Ham
- Shrimp, large, peeled
- Tuna Fish, in water
- Turkey Breast
- White Chicken Breast

DAIRY

- Cheddar Cheese (low fat)
- Cottage Cheese (low fat)
- Cream Cheese (low fat)
- Feta Cheese
- Monterrey Jack Cheese (low fat)
- Parmesan Cheese
- Eggs
- Half and half cream
- Milk, low fat
- Yogurt, low fat

HERBS/SPICES/OILS

- Baking Powder
- Basil (fresh or dried)
- Canola Oil
- Cilantro (fresh)
- Cinnamon powder
- Cumin
- Curry Powder
- Dill, (fresh or dried)

- Italian Seasoning
- Nutmeg
- Olive Oil
- Oregano, (fresh and dried)
- Parsley, Italian (fresh)
- Sage (fresh)
- Tarragon (fresh)
- Thyme (fresh and dried)
- Vanilla

CONDIMENTS

- Beef Stock
- Chicken Broth, Stock
- Coconut Milk
- Dijon Mustard
- Honey
- Light Ranch Dressing
- Maple Syrup
- Mayonnaise, low fat
- Red Wine Vinegar
- Rice Vinegar
- Soy Sauce
- Sweet Pickle Relish
- Tarragon Vinegar
- Tomato Paste
- Tomato Sauce
- Tomato Puree
- Tomato, diced, stewed (all seedless, canned)

BREAKFAST RECIPES

Apple Pancakes

Ingredients:

- 2 eggs
- 1 cup unsweetened applesauce
- 1 tsp cinnamon
- 2 tsp sugar
- 1 cup unbleached white flour
- 1/2 cup whole-wheat flour
- 2 tsp baking powder
- 2 tsp vanilla
- Non-stick cooking spray

PREPARATION:

In a medium bowl, beat eggs until fluffy. Add applesauce, cinnamon, sugar, flours, baking powder, and vanilla and continue to stir just until smooth. Heat griddle or non-stick pan over medium heat. Spray with non-stick cooking spray. For each pancake, pour slightly less than 1/4 cup batter from cup into hot pan. Cook pancakes until puffy and dry around edges. Turn and cook other side until golden. Serve pancakes with additional applesauce if desired.

SERVINGS: 4

Santa Fe Omelet

Ingredients:

- 4 large eggs
- 2 tbs water
- 1/4 tsp salt
- 1 1/2 tbs butter
- 1/2 cup red beans, canned, drained and rinsed
- 1 medium tomato, seeded, chopped
- 1/2 cup green bell pepper, seeded and chopped
- 2 tbs low fat or fat free cheddar cheese, grated
- 2 medium, round whole wheat tortillas

PREPARATION:

In a medium bowl, whisk together eggs, water and salt. Heat butter in a medium skillet and add red beans. Cook for 3 minutes, add tomatoes and green peppers. Cook for another 5 minutes until vegetables soften. Pour in egg mixture and sprinkle the cheese over the eggs. Cover until cheese melts. Serve with whole wheat tortillas.

. . .

SERVINGS: 2

Apricot Honey Oatmeal

Ingredients:

- 3 1/2 cups water
- 1/2 cup dried apricots, chopped
- 1/3 cup honey
- 1/2 tsp ground cinnamon
- 1/4 tsp salt (optional)
- 2 cups rolled oats

PREPARATION:

In a medium saucepan, bring water, apricots, honey, cinnamon and salt
to a boil. Stir in oats; return to a boil. Reduce heat to medium; cook
until most of liquid is absorbed, stirring occasionally. Serve.

SERVINGS: 4

Asparagus and Bean Frittata

Ingredients:

- 2 tsp olive oil
- 1 cup onion, chopped
- 1 cup red pepper, seeded, chopped
- 1 garlic clove, minced
- 1 (14 oz) can red beans, drained and rinsed
- 1 cup asparagus chopped and cooked
- 4 large eggs, beaten
- 1/2 tsp salt
- 1/4 cup freshly grated Parmesan cheese

PREPARATION:

Preheat oven to 350 degrees.

In a large non-stick oven proof pan, heat 1 tsp olive oil over medium-high heat. Cook onions, red peppers, garlic, and red beans until vegetables are soft (about 10 minutes).

In medium bowl, combine eggs and asparagus and salt; set aside.

Add remaining 1 tsp olive oil into pan with vegetables and add in the egg mixture. Reduce heat to medium-low and cook for 10 to 15 minutes, or until mixture is set on bottom and lightly browned. Sprinkle Parmesan cheese over top of mixture and broil for an additional 3 to 4 minutes or until cheese is lightly browned and eggs are cooked through.

SERVINGS: 4

Breakfast Blend Smoothie

Ingredients:

- 1 medium banana
- 1 cup low fat milk
- 1/2 cup yogurt, nonfat, plain
- 1/4 cup 100% bran flakes
- 1 tsp vanilla extract
- 2 tsp honey
- 1/2 cup ice
- 1 dash cinnamon or nutmeg

PREPARATION:

Combine all ingredients in a blender and process on medium speed until smooth. Garnish with cinnamon or nutmeg.

SERVINGS: 1

Broccoli Omelet

Ingredients:

- 8 large eggs
- 4 tbs water (or low fat milk)
- 1/2 tsp salt
- 1 1/2 tbs butter
- 1/2 onion, finely chopped
- 1 cup broccoli, frozen, thawed, chopped finely
- 1/2 cup Monterey jack cheese, low fat or fat free

PREPARATION:

In a bowl, whisk together eggs, water and salt. Heat butter in a medium skillet over medium-high heat, add onion and broccoli and cook until tender, about 7 minutes. Add the egg mixture, stirring to cook eggs evenly. Sprinkle with cheese. Lower heat and cover until cheese melts. Flip over in half and serve.

. . .

BARBARA CAMERON

SERVINGS: 4

Carrot and Zucchini Bread

Ingredients:

- 3 1/2 cups whole wheat flour
- 1 tbs baking powder
- 1 tsp baking soda
- 1/2 tsp salt
- 1 tsp ground cinnamon
- 2 eggs, lightly beaten
- 1 1/2 cups buttermilk
- 2 tbs butter, melted
- 1/2 cup packed brown sugar
- 1 cup shredded zucchini, unpeeled
- 1 cup shredded carrot
- 1 cup shredded apple, unpeeled

PREPARATION:

Preheat oven to 350F degrees.

Spray two 9x5-inch loaf pans with non-stick cooking spray. In a bowl, combine the flour, baking powder, baking soda, salt, and cinnamon; set aside.

In a separate bowl, combine the eggs, buttermilk, and melted butter. Stir in the brown sugar. Add the zucchini, carrots and apple and combine.

Stir in the dry ingredients into the wet ingredients and stir gently until just combined. Pour batter into prepared loaf pans. Bake for 60 minutes, or until a knife inserted into the center of the loaf comes out clean. Cool loaf in the pan for 10 minutes before removing to a wire rack to cool completely.

Multi- Grain Pancakes

Ingredients:

- 1 1/2 cups yogurt, non-fat, plain
- 1/2 cup low-fat milk
- 2 eggs
- 3 tablespoons canola oil
- 1 cup whole-wheat flour
- 1/3 cup all-purpose flour
- 1/3 cup quick cooking oats
- 2 teaspoons baking powder
- 1/2 teaspoon baking soda
- Non-stick cooking spray

PREPARATION:

In a medium bowl, combine yogurt, milk, eggs, and oil. Mix well. In a separate bowl, combine flours, oats, baking powder and soda. Mix well. Add dry ingredients to wet ingredients and mix just to moisten.

Spray a non-stick pan with non-stick cooking spray and heat pan over medium heat. For each pancake, pour slightly less than 1/4 cup batter from cup into hot pan.

Cook pancakes until puffy and dry around edges. Turn and cook other side until golden. Serve pancakes with warm maple syrup and fruit if desired.

Oatmeal Date Pancakes

Ingredients:

- 1 1/2 cups oats
- 1/2 cup whole wheat flour
- 1 tbs baking powder
- 1 tbs cinnamon
- 1 tsp nutmeg
- 1 egg
- 1 banana, mashed
- 1 tbs honey
- 1 1/2 cups milk
- 1/2 cup chopped dates
- Non-stick cooking spray

PREPARATION:

In a large bowl mix together oats, whole wheat flour, baking powder, cinnamon, and nutmeg. Set aside. In a separate bowl, mix together egg, banana, honey, milk and dates. Mix dry mixture into wet mixture.

Heat griddle or skillet over medium heat. Spray with non-stick cooking spray. For each pancake, pour slightly less than 1/4 cup batter from cup into hot griddle or pan. Cook pancakes until puffy and dry around edges. Turn and cook other side until golden.

SERVINGS: 2-3

Apple and Pear Pita Pockets

Ingredients:

- 1/2 small apple, cored, unpeeled, sliced
- 1/2 small pear, cored, unpeeled sliced
- 1/4 cup cottage cheese, low fat
- 1 round whole wheat pita bread

PREPARATION:

Combine apple, pear, and cottage cheese in a small bowl. Slice pita to make a pocket. Fill pita pocket with mixture. Serve.

SERVINGS: 1

Carrot Cake

Ingredients:

- 1 1/3 cups water
- 1 1/3 cups brown sugar
- 2 large carrots, grated
- 1 medium apple, unpeeled, chopped
- 1 teaspoon ground cinnamon
- 1 teaspoon ground cloves
- 1 teaspoon ground nutmeg
- 2 teaspoons butter
- 2 cups whole wheat flour
- 2 teaspoons baking soda
- 1 pinch salt

PREPARATION:

Preheat oven to 375F degrees. Spray a 9x5 inch loaf pan with non-stick cooking spray.

In a medium saucepan, over low heat, mix together water, sugar, carrots, apples, cinnamon, cloves, nutmeg, and butter. Cook for 5-7 minutes, until well combined, and sugar dissolves. Remove pan from heat and allow to cool.

In a large bowl, combine flour, baking soda and salt. Stir flour mixture into carrot mixture and mix just until combined. Pour into prepared pan. Bake for 1 1/4 hours, or until a knife inserted in the center comes out clean. Cool on wire racks.

Peach Breakfast Smoothie

Ingredients:

- 1/2 cup peaches, fresh or frozen
- 1 cup nonfat milk
- 1/2 cup yogurt, nonfat, peach flavored
- 1/4 cup 100% bran flakes
- 1 tsp vanilla extract
- 1 tsp honey, optional
- 1/2 cup ice

PREPARATION:

Combine all ingredients in a blender and process on high speed until smooth and creamy.

SERVINGS: 1

Peach Oatmeal

Ingredients:

- 1/2 cup rolled oats
- 3/4 cup milk or water
- 1/2 cup pureed peaches
- 1 tsp brown sugar

PREPARATION:

In a microwave-safe bowl, mix together oats, milk or water and peaches. Cook in microwave on high for 45 seconds.

Stir and microwave for another 30 seconds.

Sprinkle with brown sugar and add a splash of milk.

SERVINGS: 1

Sunrise Burrito Wrap

Ingredients:

- 1 tbs extra virgin olive oil
- 2 slices of turkey or turkey bacon
- 1/4 cup green bell peppers, seeded and chopped
- 1/4 cup black beans
- 2 eggs
- 2 tbs milk
- 1/4 tsp salt
- 2 tbs low-fat Monterrey Jack cheese, grated
- 1 whole wheat tortilla

PREPARATION:

In a small non-stick pan, heat olive oil on medium heat and cook turkey about 2 minutes until slightly crispy. Add bell peppers and beans and continue to cook until warmed through. In a small bowl beat together egg with milk and salt. Add beaten eggs and stir gently until eggs are almost cooked through. Add grated cheese and lower heat to lowest setting. Cover and continue to cook until cheese has completely melted. Place mixture on wheat tortilla and roll into a burrito.

SERVINGS: 1

Zucchini and Bean Omelet

Ingredients:

- 2 tbs extra virgin olive oil
- 1/2 cup red onions, finely chopped
- 1 medium zucchini, seeded, cubed
- 1 (14 oz) can black beans, drained and rinsed
- 1/2 medium tomato, seeded, chopped
- 4 large eggs
- 1/4 cup milk
- 1 tsp salt
- 4 whole wheat English muffins

PREPARATION:

In a large non-stick pan, heat olive oil over moderate heat.

Add onions, zucchini, black beans and tomato. Cook vegetables for 5-10 minutes or until they are soft. In a separate bowl, mix together eggs and milk and salt. Add egg mixture to pan and stir to cook through, about 5 minutes. Serve with whole wheat English muffins.

SERVINGS: 4

Banana Bran Muffins

Ingredients:

- 1 1/2 cups All-bran cereal
- 2/3 cup low fat milk
- 4 large eggs, lightly beaten
- 1/4 cup canola oil
- 1 cup ripe banana (2 medium), mashed
- 1/2 cup brown sugar
- 1 cup whole wheat flour
- 2 tsp baking powder
- 1/2 tsp salt

PREPARATION:

Preheat oven to 400F degrees.

In a large bowl, combine bran cereal and milk and set aside. Add eggs and oil; stir in mashed banana and brown sugar. In a separate small bowl, combine flour, baking powder and salt. Add dry ingredients to banana mixture, stirring just until combined. Pour batter evenly into 12 greased or paper-lined muffin tins; Bake 15 to 18 minutes or until golden-brown and firm. Allow to cool prior to serving.

SERVINGS: 12 CUPCAKES

Bran Muffins

Ingredients:

- 2 cups 100% Bran Cereal
- 1/2 cup brown sugar
- 1/2 cup butter
- 2 eggs
- 1/2 quart buttermilk
- 2 1/2 cups flour
- 2 1/2 tsp baking soda
- 1/2 tsp salt
- 1 cup dates, chopped

Preparation:

Preheat oven to 400F degrees.

Soak 1 cup of 100% Bran cereal in 1 cup boiling water and set aside. In a mixer, cream sugar and butter together until well blended. Add eggs, one at a time and beat until fluffy. Add buttermilk and soaked bran mixture.

In a separate bowl, combine flour, baking soda, and salt. Add flour mixture into the batter but do not over mix. Add in remaining 1 cup of cereal and dates. Pour batter evenly into 10 greased or paper-lined muffin tins.

Bake 15-20 minutes. Allow to cool prior to serving.

SERVINGS: 10

MAIN DISHES RECIPES

Easy Turkey Chili

Ingredients:

- 3 tbs olive oil
- 4 garlic cloves, minced
- 1 medium onion, chopped
- 1 lb. ground turkey (or lean beef)
- 1 bay leaf
- 1 tsp ground cumin
- 1 tsp dried oregano
- 1 tomato, seeded and chopped
- 1 (14 oz.) can tomato sauce
- 1 cup beef broth, store bought or homemade
- 1 tsp salt
- 2 (14 oz.) cans red beans, drained and rinsed

PREPARATION:

In a large pot, heat oil over medium heat and cook garlic and onions for a 5 minutes. Increase heat to high and add turkey, bay leaf, cumin

53

and oregano. Cook until turkey has browned, about 5-7 minutes. Add tomato, tomato sauce, broth and salt. Bring pot to a boil and then lower heat to simmer. Cover and simmer for about 20 minutes. Add beans and more water if needed, and continue to simmer for 15 more minutes. Serve.

SERVINGS: 4-6

Bean Vegetable Casserole

Ingredients:

- 3 tbs vegetable oil
- 1 large onion, chopped
- 2 stalks celery, chopped
- 1 med green bell pepper, seeded and diced
- 2 med tomatoes, seeded and diced
- 2 cups red kidney beans, drained and rinsed
- 2 1/4 cups baby lima beans, frozen and thawed
- 1 cup barley
- 2/3 cup Italian parsley, chopped
- 1/2 tsp salt
- 1 tsp dried basil
- 1/2 tsp cumin
- 1 3/4 cups boiling water

PREPARATION:

Preheat oven to 350F degrees.

In a large non-stick pan, heat oil over medium-high heat.

Add onion, celery, and green pepper. Cook for 10 minutes or until vegetables soften. Stir in tomatoes, kidney beans, lima beans, barley, parsley, salt, basil, and cumin.

Transfer mixture to a 2-to 3 quart casserole that has been sprayed with non-stick cooking spray.

Add boiling water. Cover. Bake at 350 degrees for 1-1/2 hours or until barley is tender and liquid is absorbed.

SERVINGS: 4-6

Beef and Penne Pasta

Ingredients:

- 1 lb. whole wheat penne pasta
- 1 lb ground beef lean
- 2 tbs extra virgin olive oil
- 1 small onion, chopped
- 2 garlic cloves, minced
- 1 (15 oz) can tomatoes, diced, seeded
- 2 cups green zucchini sliced to 1/4 cubes
- 8 oz. baby spinach, fresh, chopped
- 1 cup low fat parmesan cheese, grated

PREPARATION:

Bring a large pot of salted water to a boil. Cook pasta al dente according to package directions.

In a large non-stick pan, brown ground beef over medium-high heat for 6 to 8 minutes, breaking up any large pieces. Remove beef and set aside. Discard drippings.

In same pan, heat olive oil over medium-high heat. Cook onions and garlic for about 5 minutes or until soft. Add tomatoes and zucchini and continue cooking 5 minutes more. Add spinach and cook until it just wilts, 2-3 minutes. Return beef to skillet and stir in 1/2 cup cheese; heat through. Transfer pasta to a large serving bowl and spoon meat mixture on top. Toss until well combined and sprinkle with remaining cheese.

SERVINGS: 4

Black Bean Quesadillas

Ingredients:

- 1 (28 oz) can black beans, drained and rinsed
- 1/2 cup tomatoes, seeded and chopped
- 3 tbs cilantro, chopped
- 1/2 cup black olives, pitted, halved
- 1/2 tsp cumin
- 1/2 cup low fat or fat free Monterey Jack cheese, shredded
- 2 cups fresh spinach leaves, shredded
- 8 round whole wheat tortillas

PREPARATION:

Preheat oven to 350 degrees.

In a bowl, mash beans until smooth, but, slightly chunky. Stir in tomato, cilantro and olives and cumin. Spread mixture evenly onto 4 tortillas. Sprinkle with cheese, and spinach. Top with remaining tortillas.

Bake tortillas on ungreased cookie sheet for 12 minutes. Cut into wedges and serve.

SERVINGS: 4

Broccoli and Mushroom Rice

Ingredients:

- 1 tbs extra virgin olive oil
- 1 medium onion, chopped
- 2 cloves garlic, minced
- 1 cup instant brown rice
- 8 oz. Portobello mushroom, sliced
- 3/4 cup vegetable broth, store bought or homemade
- 1 lb fresh broccoli florets
- 1/2 tsp salt

PREPARATION:

Preheat oven to 350F degrees.

In a non-stick pan, heat olive oil over medium- high heat. Cook onions and garlic until soft, about 5 minutes. Stir in rice and mushrooms and cook 3-5 minutes or until mushrooms have released all of their juices. Add the broth and bring to a boil. Reduce heat to medium-low and cover until liquid is absorbed (about 7 - 8 minutes). Place broccoli in a microwave safe casserole dish and sprinkle with salt and add 4 tbs. water. Cover and cook at high power for 5 to 7 minutes or until tender. Place rice into a serving platter and top with broccoli. Toss to combine and serve.

SERVINGS: 4

Chicken and Lentil Pita

Ingredients:

- 1 cup fat free cream cheese, softened
- 1 tbs low fat or fat free mayonnaise
- 2 cups cooked chicken, cubed
- 1 cup tomatoes, seeded, sliced
- 1 (14 oz) can lentils, cooked
- 4 romaine lettuce leaves
- 2 cups alfalfa sprouts, rinsed, drained
- 4 round whole wheat pita bread

PREPARATION:

In a medium bowl, combine cream cheese and mayonnaise until well blended. Add chicken, tomatoes, lentils; mix well. Slice the pita bread to form a pocket. Place lettuce inside and fill each pita with the chicken mixture. Top with alfalfa sprouts. Serve.

. . .

SERVINGS: 4

Chicken and Asparagus Pasta

Ingredients:

- 1 lb. whole wheat penne pasta
- 2 tbs olive oil
- 3/4 lb chicken breast halves, sliced into strips
- 1/2 tsp poultry seasoning (thyme, marjoram, basil)
- 4 cloves garlic, minced
- 1 1/2 cup asparagus, frozen, thawed cut into 1 inch pieces
- 1 cup peas, frozen, thawed
- 1/4 cup parmesan cheese, grated

PREPARATION:

Bring a large pot of salted water to boil. Add pasta and cook al dente according to package directions. Heat one tablespoon olive oil in a non-stick pan over medium heat and cook chicken with poultry seasoning until golden. Remove cooked chicken from the pan. Add the remaining tablespoon of olive oil, garlic, asparagus and peas. Cook until vegetables are tender. Place chicken back in with the asparagus mixture and cook together for 2 minutes or until heated through. Place pasta in a large shallow pasta bowl and toss with chicken mixture. Top with parmesan cheese.

SERVINGS: 4

Chicken and Avocado Pitas

Ingredients:

- 2 cups chicken, cooked, cubed
- 1 medium avocado, chopped
- 1 (14 oz.) can red beans, drained and rinsed
- 1 tsp lemon juice
- 1 cup tomatoes, seeded, chopped
- 1 cup low fat cottage cheese
- 4 round whole wheat pita bread

PREPARATION:

In a large mixing bowl, combine chicken, avocado, red beans, lemon juice, tomatoes, and cottage cheese. Slice the pita bread to make a pocket and spoon in the chicken mixture. Serve.

SERVINGS: 4

Apple Chicken Pita

Ingredients:

- 2 cups cooked chicken, cubed
- 2 medium apples, unpeeled, chopped
- 1 celery stalk, chopped
- 1/3 cup plain yogurt, low fat or non-fat
- 1/4 cup mayonnaise, non-fat
- 4 round whole wheat pita breads
- 4 romaine lettuce leaves

PREPARATION:

In a medium bowl, combine the chicken, apples, and celery.

Add yogurt and mayonnaise. Mix well. Slice pita to make a pocket. Line with lettuce leaf and fill pita pocket with 1 cup of mixture per pita bread. Serve with mixed fruit salad (no berries).

. . .

SERVINGS: 4

Chicken Florentine

Ingredients:

- 2 tbs olive oil
- 2 medium zucchinis, seeded, thinly sliced
- 1/2 cups green onions, sliced
- 2 cups chicken breast, cubed
- 1/2 tsp salt
- 1/2 tsp thyme, ground
- 2 tbs pimento, chopped
- 3 cups cooked long-grain rice
- 4 cups fresh baby spinach washed and dried
- 1/4 cup low fat parmesan cheese, freshly grated

PREPARATION:

In a non-stick pan, heat olive oil over moderate heat. Add zucchini, onions, and chicken, stirring occasionally for 5 to 10 minutes, or until chicken is golden. Add salt, thyme, pimento, rice and spinach. Cook and stir for another 6 - 8 minutes or until heated through and spinach wilts. Remove from heat, transfer to large serving bowl, and stir in cheese. Serve.

SERVINGS: 4

Chipotle Black Bean Chili

Ingredients:

- 1 tbs olive oil
- 1 cup onion, finely chopped
- 4 cloves garlic, minced
- 1/2 tsp chipotle powder
- 1/2 tsp cumin
- 1/4 tsp salt
- 1 (30 oz) can black beans, drained and rinsed
- 1 (28 oz) can diced and seedless tomatoes
- 1 tsp fresh cilantro

PREPARATION:

In a large non-stick pan, heat olive oil over medium heat. Add onions and garlic and cook 5 minutes or until they are soft. Add chipotle powder, cumin, salt, beans, and tomatoes bring to a boil. Reduce heat, cover and simmer 15-25 or until chili thickens. Garnish with fresh cilantro. Serve.

. . .

SERVINGS: 4

Cottage Crunch Wraps

Ingredients:

- 3/4 cup cottage cheese
- 1/4 cup carrots, grated
- 1/4 cup green onions, sliced finely
- 1/2 cup tomatoes, seeded and chopped
- 1/2 cup cabbage, chopped
- 1 teaspoon lime juice
- 2 round whole wheat tortillas

PREPARATION:

In a medium bowl, place cheese, carrots, onions, tomatoes, and cabbage and mix well. Add lime juice. Place mixture in tortillas, wrap and serve.

SERVINGS: 2

Bean Enchiladas

Ingredients:

- 1 (14 oz) can red beans, drained rinsed and mashed
- 2 cups low- fat or fat free cheddar cheese, shredded
- 1/2 cup onion, chopped
- 1/4 cup black olives, sliced
- 2 cups tomato sauce
- 2 tsp garlic salt
- 8 medium whole wheat tortillas

PREPARATION:

Preheat oven to 350F degrees.

In a medium bowl, combine the mashed beans, cheese, onions, olives, one cup tomato sauce, and garlic salt. Place about 1/3 cup bean mixture along center of each tortilla. Roll up and place enchiladas in large baking dish. Spoon remaining tomato sauce on top of the filled tortillas. Sprinkle with additional cheese, if desired. Bake for 15 to 20 minutes or until thoroughly heated.

SERVINGS: 4

Couscous with Chicken

Ingredients:

- 4 tbs extra-virgin olive oil
- 1 lb boneless, skinless chicken thighs, chopped
- 1 onion, chopped
- 3 cloves garlic, minced
- 1 cup shredded carrots
- 1 tsp smoked paprika, cumin
- 1/8 tsp ground cinnamon
- 1/2 tsp salt
- 1 cup chopped dried fruits, (pitted dates, apricots)
- 4 cups chicken stock, divided (store bought or homemade)
- 2 tablespoons butter
- 1 1/2 cups couscous
- 1/2 cup Italian parsley, chopped

PREPARATION:

In a large pan, heat oil over medium-high heat. Cook chicken and brown 3 to 4 minutes on each side. Add onions, garlic, carrots, and season with spices and salt. Cook 6-8 minutes. Stir the fruits into the chicken and vegetables, and 2 1/2 cups of stock. Allow to boil. Reduce heat to low, cover and simmer 10 minutes. In a separate small saucepan, over medium heat, pour 1 1/2 cups stock and bring up to a boil then stir in couscous. Remove from heat, cover and let stand 5 minutes. Fluff with fork and serve with chicken.

SERVINGS: 4

Beef Fajitas

Ingredients:

- 5 oz flank steak, trimmed of excess fat
- 2 tsp lime juice
- 1 tsp garlic, chopped
- 1 tsp extra virgin olive oil, divided
- 1 (15 oz) can red beans, drained and rinsed
- 1/2 cup green bell pepper, thinly sliced
- 1/2 cup red bell pepper, thinly sliced
- 1 tbsp scallions, chopped finely
- Salt to taste
- 4 whole wheat tortillas

PREPARATION:

Season flank steak with salt. Let sit for 10 minutes. Grill flank steak over high heat until cooked on both sides. Place steak on separate plate to rest for 10 minutes. Cut flank steak into thin strips against the grain. In a small bowl, whisk together lime juice, garlic, and olive oil. Set aside.

In a separate bowl, combine beans, bell peppers and scallions and season with salt. To assemble fajitas, take tortilla and place steak inside. Top with bean mixture and drizzle some of the lime sauce on top. Roll into fajita and serve immediately.

SERVINGS: 4 FAJITAS

Couscous with Dates

Ingredients:

- 1/2 cup water
- 1 cup chicken stock, store bought or homemade
- 1tbs olive oil
- 1/2 cup dried dates, chopped
- 1 cup couscous
- 1 cup leafy greens (spinach, or escarole), chopped
- 1/2 tsp lemon juice
- 1/2 tsp salt

PREPARATION:

In a medium saucepan, over high heat, bring water, chicken broth, oil and dates to a boil. Remove from heat and stir in couscous. Cover and let sit for 5-10 minutes.

Stir in spinach into couscous. Add lemon juice and salt and fluff together with a fork. Serve.

. . .

SERVINGS: 4

Couscous with Vegetables

Ingredients:

- 1 1/2 cups of chicken broth
- 1 cup couscous, plain
- 4 tbs olive oil, divided
- 1 red onion, chopped
- 2 cloves garlic, minced
- 3 large tomatoes, seeded and diced
- 1 yellow bell pepper, seeded and chopped
- 1 red bell pepper, seeded and chopped
- 2 zucchinis, seeded and chopped
- 1 cup peas, frozen and thawed
- 2 tbs balsamic vinegar
- 2 tbs feta cheese, crumbled

PREPARATION:

In a medium saucepan, over high heat, bring chicken broth and 1 tbs of olive oil to a boil. Remove from heat and stir in couscous. Cover and let sit for 5-10 minutes.

In a separate pan over medium heat, add the remaining oil and cook the onions and garlic until softened. Mix in the tomatoes, bell peppers and zucchinis. Cook and stir until tender. Add peas and cook 2-3 more minutes. Add vinegar and cheese and toss to combine. Pour the vegetable mixture over couscous. Serve.

SERVINGS: 4

Easy Beef Stir Fry

Ingredients:

- 1/4 cup orange juice
- 1/4 cup low-sodium soy sauce
- 2 tbsp rice vinegar
- 1/4 cup water
- 2 tbsp canola oil
- 8 oz beef round tip steak, sliced thinly
- 2 cloves garlic, minced
- 6 oz cups peas, frozen and thawed
- 1 large bunch broccoli florets, fresh (or frozen and thawed)
- 8 oz shelled edamame, frozen and thawed
- 1 1/2 tsp cornstarch dissolved in 1/4 cup warm water

PREPARATION:

In a small bowl, combine orange juice, soy sauce, rice vinegar, and water until well combined. Set aside.

In a large non-stick pan, heat 1 tablespoon of canola oil over medium-high heat. Add the beef and cook, stirring, until just browned, about 2 minutes. Transfer the beef to a separate plate. Heat another tablespoon of oil over medium heat and cook garlic about 1 minute, without burning it. Add peas, broccoli and edamame, and continue to cook for 3 minutes. Add the soy sauce mixture and cook, stirring, until broccoli is cooked and crisp-tender, about 5 minutes. Add the sliced beef back into pan and add dissolved cornstarch in water and stir to combine all ingredients. Cook until mixture thickens slightly and beef is heated through. Serve immediately.

SERVINGS: 2-3

Grilled Fish Tacos

Ingredients:

- 1/4 tsp salt
- Juice of 1/2 lemon
- 2 tbs olive oil
- 4 fish filets, such as trout or tilapia, rinsed and dried
- 1/2 cup red onion, chopped
- 1/2 cup jicama, peeled, chopped
- 1/3 cup red bell pepper, chopped
- 2/3 cup fresh cilantro, finely chopped
- 1 cup black beans, drained and rinsed
- Zest and juice of 1/2 lime
- 1 tbs plain yogurt, non-fat
- 8 whole wheat tortillas, warmed

PREPARATION:

In a small bowl, combine salt, lemon juice, and olive oil. Pour mixture over fish fillets and let marinate for 10 minutes. Grill fish over high heat until cooked through, about 3 minutes per side. In a separate bowl, combine onion, jicama, bell pepper, cilantro, beans, zest and juice of lime and yogurt to make a "salsa". To make tacos, place fish in warmed tortilla and cover with "salsa" and fold in half. Serve.

SERVINGS: 4

Ham, Bean and Cabbage Stew

Ingredients:

- 1 tbs extra virgin olive oil
- 8 oz smoked ham, chopped
- 1 large onion, chopped
- 2 stalks celery, sliced
- 5 cloves garlic, chopped finely
- 4 cups chicken broth
- 1 (28 oz) can tomatoes, seedless, drained
- 3 cups whole wheat pasta
- 8 oz readymade coleslaw
- 2 (14 oz) cans kidney beans
- 1 tsp dried basil
- 1tsp dried rosemary

PREPARATION:

In a large pot, heat olive oil over medium heat. Cook ham, onion, celery and garlic stirring occasionally, until vegetables are tender. Stir in broth and tomatoes, breaking up tomatoes. Stir in pasta, heat to boiling and reduce heat to low. Cover and simmer about 10 minutes or until pasta is tender. Stir in coleslaw, beans, basil and oregano. Bring stew to a boil and reduce heat to low. Simmer uncovered about 5-7 minutes or until cabbage is tender.

SERVINGS: 4

Garbanzo Pita Pockets

Ingredients:

- 1 (15 oz) can garbanzo beans, drained and rinsed
- 1 (6 oz) can artichoke hearts, marinated, quartered, liquid reserved
- 1 tbs black olives, sliced
- 1 tbs green olives, sliced
- 1 small green bell pepper, seeded and diced
- 1 small red bell pepper, seeded and diced
- 1 small red onion, thinly sliced
- 2 tbs red wine vinegar
- 1/2 cup basil, fresh and chopped
- 4 large whole wheat pita bread
- 4 leaves lettuce

PREPARATION:

In a large bowl, combine the garbanzo beans, artichokes and their liquid, olives, garlic, peppers, onion, vinegar and basil. Mix well and set aside. Slice pita bread to make a pocket. Place a lettuce leaf in each pita and fill with the garbanzo filling. Serve.

SERVINGS: 4

Grilled Steak with Spinach and Apple Salad

Ingredients:

- 2 beef steaks (rib-eye or sirloin)
- 4 tbs extra virgin olive oil
- Salt to taste
- 1 tbs balsamic vinegar
- 2 cups fresh baby spinach, washed and dried
- 1 Granny smith or other tart apple, unpeeled, sliced
- 4 oz fresh Parmesan cheese, grated or cut into very thin strips

PREPARATION:

Prepare steaks for grill by pouring 2 tbs olive oil and salt to taste. Grill over high heat to desired doneness, about 7 minutes per side for medium. Once cooked, place steaks on plate to rest and let juices redistribute without cutting.

To make dressing, in a small bowl, whisk together balsamic vinegar, 2 tbs olive oil and salt to taste.

On individual plates, stack spinach, apples and steak that have been cut diagonally. Drizzle with dressing and top with Parmesan cheese.

SERVINGS: 2

Grilled Vegetable Sandwich

Ingredients:

- 1 Japanese eggplant, sliced in half-inch thick slices
- 1 small zucchini, sliced in half-inch thick slices
- 1 red pepper, seeded and quartered
- 2 Portobello mushroom caps
- 1/2 cup extra-virgin olive oil
- 1/4 tsp salt
- 1 cup goat cheese (6 oz), plain
- 8 slices whole wheat baguette or other crusty bread
- 1 cup baby spinach, divided into 4 equal parts

PREPARATION:

With a pastry brush, brush olive oil on the vegetable slices and the mushrooms caps. Season them with salt. Place vegetables on a hot grill and cook until they are tender. To assemble, slice mushrooms into 1/4-inch slices, spread both sides of the bread with goat cheese and then top with 1 slice each of grilled vegetables and a quarter of the mushrooms. Top with spinach and remaining piece of bread. Serve.

SERVINGS: 4

Grilled Vegetable Quesadillas

Ingredients:

- 1 small zucchini
- 1 small yellow squash
- 1 small yellow onion
- 1 red pepper, seeded
- 1 small Portobello mushroom
- 1/2 tsp oregano
- 1/4 tsp salt
- 2 tortillas, spinach or whole wheat
- 1/2 cup low fat or non-fat Mozzarella cheese, shredded

PREPARATION:

Grill vegetables over medium heat until all of the vegetables are cooked. Season with oregano and salt. Slice vegetables and toss together. Heat a non-stick pan sprayed with non-stick cooking spray over medium heat and place one tortilla in the pan. Spread some of the vegetable mixture over the tortilla, sprinkle with cheese and top with the remaining tortilla. Turn tortilla over and heat the other side until cheese melts but do not brown the tortillas. Serve.

SERVINGS: 2 -4

Lentil Risotto

Ingredients:

- 2 tbs. olive oil
- 4 medium leeks, chopped
- 3 cloves garlic, minced
- 1 medium red pepper, seeded, finely chopped
- 3 cups chicken broth, store bought or homemade
- 1 1/4 cup long grain rice
- 1 tbs basil, chopped
- 1 cup lentils, cooked
- 1/4 cup fresh Italian parsley, chopped
- 1/4 cup fresh parmesan cheese, grated

PREPARATION:

In a large pot, heat olive oil over moderate heat and cook leeks, garlic, and red pepper until softened. Add broth along with the rice, and basil. Cover and let simmer until rice is done then add cooked lentils and stir for 10 minutes. Remove from heat and add parsley and parmesan cheese. Serve.

SERVINGS: 4

Lentil Stew

Ingredients:

- 1 tbs vegetable oil
- 1 large onion, chopped
- 2 cloves garlic, finely chopped
- 1 med green bell pepper, chopped
- 3 cups water (or broth)
- 1 1/4 cups lentils, uncooked, rinsed
- 1 can tomato sauce
- ½ tsp oregano
- ½ tsp thyme
- ½ tsp basil
- ½ tsp paprika

PREPARATION:

In a large saucepan, heat oil over medium-high heat. Cook onion, garlic, and bell pepper, stirring frequently, until vegetables are tender.

Stir in water, lentils, tomato sauce and spices. Reduce heat to low and partially cover and simmer 35 to 40 minutes or until lentils are tender. Serve.

SERVINGS: 4

Lentil Spaghetti Stew

Ingredients:

- 3 tbs olive oil
- 1 large onion, chopped
- 4 cloves garlic, minced
- 3 carrots, chopped
- 3 celery stalks, chopped
- 1 cup lentils, uncooked
- 2 1/2 quarts water, more if needed
- 2 tsp salt
- 1 leaf bay leaf
- 1/4 lb linguine, broken into 1 1/2-inch pieces
- 2 cups kale (or Swiss chard), chopped
- 1/2 cup fresh Italian parsley, chopped

PREPARATION:

In a large pot, heat olive oil over moderate heat. Cook the onion, garlic, and carrots and celery for 10 minutes, stirring occasionally, until tender.

Add the lentils, water, salt, and bay leaf to the pot. Bring to a boil. Reduce the heat and simmer, partially covered, stirring occasionally, for 15 minutes. Add the linguine and simmer, stirring occasionally, until the lentils are tender and the pasta and kale are tender, 15 to 20 minutes longer. Stir parsley into the stew. Serve.

SERVINGS: 4

Lentil Stir Fry

Ingredients:

- 1 cup sugar snap peas
- 2 tbs olive oil
- 1 small onion, chopped
- 8 oz. mushrooms, sliced
- 1 (8 oz) can artichoke hearts, drained
- 1 (8 oz) can green lentils, drained
- 4 tbs half and half cream
- 1/2 tsp salt

PREPARATION:

Bring a saucepan of salted water to boil. Add sugar snap peas and set aside for 4 minutes until tender. Drain under cold water and pat dry with paper towel. Set aside.

In a medium pan, heat olive oil and cook onions for 2-3 minutes. Add sliced mushrooms and stir for 2-3 minutes. Add the peas, artichoke hearts, and lentils to the pan. Stir-fry for 2 minutes. Stir in the cream and salt and cook for 1 minute. Serve.

SERVINGS: 4

Mushroom and Bean Stew

Ingredients:

- 2 tbs olive oil
- 1 lb white mushrooms, sliced
- 1 cup onions, chopped
- 1 tsp garlic, minced
- 3/4 tsp dried thyme
- 2 (14 oz) cans chicken broth
- 1 (14 oz) can stewed tomatoes, chopped
- 1/4 cup dry white wine
- 2 (15 oz)cans cannellini beans

PREPARATION:

In a large saucepan, heat olive oil over medium high heat. Cook mushrooms, onion, garlic and thyme until onion is tender and mushrooms are slightly golden (about 7 minutes). Add chicken broth, tomatoes and wine and bring to a boil. Cover and simmer for about 15 additional minutes. In a small bowl, mash 1 cup of the beans until smooth; add to stew. Stir in remaining beans, heat until hot. Serve immediately with a side of cooked long grain rice, if desired.

SERVINGS: 4

Spaghetti with Zucchini

Ingredients:

- 1 lb whole wheat spaghetti
- 2 medium zucchini, grated, water squeezed out
- 2 tbs butter
- 1 tbs olive oil
- 2 cloves garlic, minced
- 1/2 cup Parmesan cheese, freshly grated

PREPARATION:

Bring a large pot of salted water to boil. Add pasta and cook according to package directions until al dente. While pasta

cooks, in a large non-stick pan, heat butter and oil together. Add grated zucchini and cook for about 3 minutes. Add garlic and cook for one more minute, stirring constantly. Add 1/4 cup of grated parmesan cheese. Place pasta in a large shallow pasta bowl and toss in zucchini mixture. Top with remaining parmesan cheese. Serve.

. . .

SERVINGS: 4

Roasted Chicken and Vegetables

Ingredients:

- 6 Roma tomatoes, seedless, quartered
- 3 medium zucchini, chopped coarsely
- 2 large potatoes, unpeeled, quartered
- 3 tbs olive oil, divided
- 3/4 tsp salt, divided
- 4 cloves garlic, finely minced
- 1 tbs fresh rosemary, chopped
- 1 tbs fresh thyme, leaves taken off sprig
- 1 tsp lemon zest
- 1 tbs lemon juice
- 4 chicken breast halves skinless

PREPARATION:

Preheat oven to 375F degrees.

Place tomatoes, zucchini and potatoes in a large roasting pan, and toss with 2 tbs of oil and 1/4 tsp salt. In a small bowl, combine 1 tbs oil, 1/2 tsp salt, garlic, rosemary, thyme, lemon zest and lemon juice. Pour this mixture over chicken. Place chicken in pan with vegetables. Bake in oven for 30 minutes. Stir chicken and vegetables and bake another 25 minutes, or until chicken is cooked through and vegetables are tender.

SERVINGS: 4

Pasta with Chicken and Olives

Ingredients:

- 1 lb whole wheat pasta, uncooked
- 2 tsp olive oil
- 1 large onion, peeled, chopped finely
- 4 cloves garlic, peeled, finely chopped
- 1 lb chicken breast, cut into chunks
- 1 tsp basil, dried
- 1 tsp rosemary, dried
- 12 med black olives, pitted
- 1 med green bell pepper, seeded and chopped
- 1 (14 oz) can tomatoes, seedless, chopped
- 1 can chicken broth, store bought or homemade
- 1/2 cup Romano cheese, shredded

PREPARATION:

Bring a large pot of salted water to boil. Add pasta and cook according to package directions until al dente. While pasta cooks, heat the oil in a large pan over medium heat. Add the onion and garlic and cook until the onion is tender, about 6 minutes. Add the chicken, basil and rosemary and cook until the chicken is lightly browned, about 8 minutes. Stir in the olives, green pepper and tomatoes and cook until the tomatoes begin to give off liquid, about 2 minutes.

Add the chicken broth to the pan, heat pan to boiling and boil until half of the liquid is evaporated, about 5-7 minutes. When pasta is done, add to sauce mixture. Toss until pasta is evenly mixed with sauce. Top with cheese and serve.

SERVINGS: 4

Pasta with Escarole, Beans and Turkey

Ingredients:

- 3/4 pound whole-wheat bowtie pasta
- 1 tbs olive oil
- 1/2 medium onion, chopped
- 3 cloves garlic, minced
- 6 oz turkey, ground
- 1 medium head escarole, rinsed, drained and chopped,
- 1(14oz) can cannellini beans, drained and rinsed
- 1 1/2 cups chicken broth
- 1 tbs fresh rosemary, chopped
- 1/2 tsp salt
- 1/4 cup Parmesan cheese, grated

PREPARATION:

Bring a large pot of salted water to boil. Add pasta and cook according to package directions. Drain. In a large non-stick pan, heat olive oil over medium heat. Add onion and cook until softened, add garlic and turkey and cook until it browns, about 5 minutes. Add the escarole and cook until wilted, about 3 to 4 minutes. Add the beans, 1 cup of chicken stock, rosemary, and salt. Simmer until the mixture is slightly thickened. Add the turkey-bean mixture to pasta and toss well, thinning sauce with the additional 1/2 cup chicken stock if necessary. Top with parmesan cheese. Serve.

SERVINGS: 4

Pasta with White Beans, Tomato and Feta

Ingredients:

- 1 lb whole wheat penne pasta
- 2 tbs olive oil
- 2 cloves garlic, minced
- 3 cups tomatoes, seeded and chopped
- 1 (14 oz) can cannellini beans, drained and rinsed
- 1 cup tomato sauce
- 2 cups fresh spinach washed and chopped
- 1/2 cup crumbled feta cheese

PREPARATION:

Bring a large pot of salted water to a boil. Add pasta and cook according to package instructions. Drain. In a large non-stick pan, heat olive oil over medium heat. Cook garlic for 3 - 4 minutes. Add tomatoes, beans and tomato sauce. Bring to a boil. Reduce heat, cover and let simmer for 10 minutes. Add spinach to the sauce and let simmer for another 5 minutes or until spinach wilts. Place cooked pasta in a large serving bowl, pour sauce over pasta and sprinkle feta cheese. Toss to combine. Serve.

SERVINGS: 4

Tofu Stir Fry

Ingredients:

- 1 (14 oz) pkg. firm tofu, drained, cut in cubes
- 1/4 cup whole wheat flour
- 1 tbs canola oil
- 1/2 cup olive oil
- 2 tbs balsamic vinegar
- 1 tbs Dijon mustard
- 3 tbs soy sauce
- 1/2 cup onions, sliced
- 1/2 cups carrots, sliced
- 1 cup green beans, ends cut,
- 1/2 cups fresh soy beans
- 1 1/2 cups cabbage, chopped
- 1 cup brown rice, cooked

PREPARATION:

In a shallow bowl or plate, mix tofu with flour until evenly coated. In a non-stick pan, heat canola oil over medium-high heat. Add tofu and cook until lightly brown. Remove from pan and put aside. Prepare dressing by whisking together olive oil, vinegar, mustard and soy sauce. In same pan, combine 2 tablespoons of the dressing mixture with onions, carrots, green beans, soy beans and cabbage. Stir fry for 10 minutes or until vegetables are tender. Add remaining dressing mixture and tofu. Mix. Cook for 2 minutes, stirring gently. Serve over hot brown rice.

SERVINGS: 4

Quick Broccoli Pasta

Ingredients:

- 2 cups broccoli florets, fresh (or frozen and thawed)
- 1/2 lb whole wheat pasta
- 1/2 tbs extra virgin olive oil
- 1 1/2 tbs parmesan cheese, grated
- 1/8 tsp garlic powder

PREPARATION:

Bring a large pot of salted water to a boil. Add broccoli and pasta and cook for about 6 - 8 minutes or until tender. Drain well. Place pasta mixture in a large shallow pasta bowl and toss with olive oil, cheese and garlic powder. Serve.

SERVINGS: 2

Red Beans and Rice

Ingredients:

- 1 tbs olive oil
- 1 medium onion, chopped
- 2 sticks celery, chopped
- 2 cloves garlic, chopped
- 1 (14 oz) can tomato paste
- 1/2 tsp oregano
- 1/2 tsp thyme
- 1(14 oz) can beef stock, store bought or homemade
- 1 (28 oz) can red beans, drained and rinsed

PREPARATION:

In a large non-stick pan, heat olive oil over medium heat. Cook onions, celery and garlic stirring until just tender. Stir in tomato paste, oregano and thyme. Add beef broth, stir and bring to a boil. Simmer uncovered about 15 minutes or until mixture thickens. Add red beans and let cook until heated through. Serve over rice.

. . .

SERVINGS: 4-6

Rice Bowl with Shrimp and Peas

Ingredients:

- 1 cup long-grain brown rice
- 1/4 cup soy sauce
- 1/4 cup fresh lemon juice
- 2 tbs rice vinegar
- 2 tbs honey
- 1 tbs olive oil
- 1 lb medium shrimp, cleaned, peeled, deveined
- 8 oz snow peas, thawed if frozen, cut in halves
- 1 (1-inch long) piece fresh ginger shredded
- 1 Hass avocado, chopped

PREPARATION:

In a large saucepan, bring 2 cups of water to a boil. Add the rice and cover and reduce heat to simmer. Cook until rice is tender and water has evaporated, about 35-45 minutes.

While rice is cooking, in a small bowl, combine soy sauce, lemon juice, vinegar, and honey until well combined.

In a large non-stick pan, heat olive oil over medium-high heat. Cook shrimp with peas and ginger until shrimp turn pink, about 3 minutes.

To serve, place rice on plate and top with shrimp mixture and chopped avocado. Serve the sauce on the side.

SERVINGS: 4

Rice and Vegetable Casserole

Ingredients:

- Non-stick cooking spray
- 1 cup long-grain brown rice
- 1/4 cup fresh mushrooms, sliced
- 1/4 cup broccoli, chopped
- 1/4 cup carrots, chopped
- 1/4 cup red bell pepper, seeded and chopped
- 1/4 cup onion, finely chopped
- 1 tsp salt
- 1 tsp paprika
- 1 tsp oregano
- 2 -1/2 cups vegetable broth, store bought or homemade
- 1/4 cup low fat or fat free cheddar cheese, shredded

PREPARATION:

Preheat oven to 425 degrees.

Spray a 13x9 glass baking dish lightly with non-stick cooking spray.

In a large bowl, combine brown rice, mushrooms, broccoli, carrots, bell pepper, onion, salt, paprika, oregano and broth. Mix well and cover with foil. Bake in preheated oven for 30 minutes, or until cooked through; stir once half way during baking. Top with shredded cheddar cheese and allow it to melt prior to serving.

SERVINGS: 4

Savory Rice with Lentils

Ingredients:

- 2 tbs. olive oil
- 1 onion, chopped
- 2 carrots, finely chopped
- 1 bell pepper, chopped (red or green)
- 1 garlic clove, minced
- 1 tbs dried basil
- 1 tsp dried sage
- 1 cup brown rice
- 3 cups chicken broth, store bought or homemade
- 1 cup lentils, uncooked and rinsed

PREPARATION:

In a large pan, heat olive oil over medium-high heat. Cook onion, carrot and pepper until softened, about 5-7 minutes. Add garlic and cook for one more minute. Add basil, sage and rice. Stir to combine.

Stir in broth. Bring to a boil, stirring occasionally. Add lentils. Cover and reduce heat to low and let simmer for 20-25 minutes. Fluff with fork and serve.

SERVES 6

Shrimp and Black Bean Nachos

Ingredients:

- 3/4 cup cilantro, fresh chopped
- 1/2 cup red onion, diced
- 2 tbs fresh lime juice
- 1 tbs olive oil
- 1 tsp Worcestershire sauce
- 1/2 tsp salt
- 3/4 lb medium shrimp, peeled, cooked, and chopped
- 2 cups tomatoes, seeded, diced
- 1/2 cup avocado, diced
- 1 (15 oz) can black beans, drained and rinsed
- 1/2 tsp ground cumin
- 4 cup baked tortilla chips

Preparation:

Combine cilantro, onion, lime juice, oil, Worcestershire sauce, salt and shrimp in a large bowl; toss well. Cover and refrigerate for 30 minutes. Add tomato and avocado; stir well.

Place the beans and cumin in a food processor, and process 30 seconds or until smooth. Spread each chip with 1-teaspoon black-bean mixture. Top with 1-tablespoon shrimp mixture.

Serve.

SERVINGS: 4

Southwestern Chicken Pitas

Ingredients:

- 1 (15 oz) can black beans, drained, rinsed
- 1/2 cup red bell pepper, chopped, seeded
- 3 tbs fresh lime juice
- 2 tbs fresh cilantro leaves, minced
- 2 tbs canola oil
- 4 chicken breasts, boneless, halved, skinless
- 4 round whole wheat pita bread
- 6 slices low-fat provolone cheese, cut in halves

PREPARATION:

In a bowl, combine beans, bell pepper, lime juice, and cilantro. Set aside. In a large pan, heat canola oil over medium-high heat. Cook chicken in pan until golden brown. Set aside for 10 without cutting. Warm pita bread in oven. Cut chicken into slices. For each sandwich, place cheese slice halves down center of one pita bread. Top with chicken breast slices and bean mixture. Roll up tightly. Cut in half and serve.

SERVINGS: 6

Spinach and Ham Pizza

Ingredients:

- 1 store-bought baked thin-crust whole wheat pizza shell
- 4 cups baby spinach leaves, thinly sliced
- 2 teaspoons olive oil
- 3 ounces ham, thinly sliced, or prosciutto
- 1/4 Feta cheese, crumbled
- 1/4 cup grated Parmesan cheese
- 3 cloves thinly sliced garlic

PREPARATION:

Preheat oven to 450F degrees.

Place the pizza shell on a cookie sheet. Scatter spinach all over crust. Drizzle with oil. Place ham or prosciutto, cheeses, and garlic on top of spinach. Bake for 10-12 minutes, until spinach is wilted.

. . .

SERVINGS: 4

Ziti with Zesty Chicken

Ingredients:

- 1 lb whole wheat pasta, (ziti or bowtie)
- 2 tsp olive oil
- 1 medium onion, chopped
- 1 tbs Dijon mustard
- 2 tbs whole wheat flour
- 2 cups chicken broth
- 1/4 cup lemon juice
- 12 oz peas, frozen and thawed
- 1/4 cup fresh Italian parsley, chopped
- 12 oz cooked chicken, chopped

PREPARATION:

Bring a large pot of salted water to a boil. Add pasta and cook according to package instructions until al dente. While pasta is cooking, in a large non-stick pan, heat olive oil over medium heat. Add the onion and cook for 3 minutes. Stir in the Dijon mustard and flour. Gradually whisk in the chicken broth, stirring constantly to avoid clumps. Bring the broth to a boil and stir in the lemon juice, peas and parsley. Add cooked pasta and cooked chicken to sauce and serve.

SERVINGS: 4

Summer Spaghetti

Ingredients:

- 1 lb whole wheat spaghetti
- 1/4 cup olive oil
- 1 shallot, minced
- 2 cloves garlic, minced
- 1 medium zucchini, chopped
- 1 medium summer squash, chopped
- 1/2 lb green beans, ends cut
- 1/4 cup fresh basil, coarsely chopped
- 1/2 tsp salt
- 1/2 medium lemon, juiced
- 2 tbs unsalted butter, room temperature
- freshly grated lemon peel

PREPARATION:

Bring a large pot of salted water to boil. Add pasta and cook according to package directions until al dente.

In a large pan, heat oil over medium heat and cook the shallot and garlic stirring frequently.

Add the zucchini, squash, green beans, and basil. Continue to cook, stirring occasionally, until all vegetables are tender. Season vegetables with salt and lemon juice. Immediately place the sautéed vegetables with all their juices in a large shallow pasta bowl. Add the linguine and butter, toss to mix well and serve immediately.

SERVINGS: 4

Tortellini in Navy Bean Sauce

❦

Ingredients:

- 2 cups navy or white beans, uncooked
- 2 tbs olive oil
- 1 small onion, chopped
- 2 garlic cloves, finely chopped
- 1 cup tomatoes, seeded and chopped
- 2 tbs tomato paste
- 7 cups chicken broth, store bought or homemade
- 1 bay leaf
- 1 lb tortellini, store bought, with the filling of your choice
- 1/4 cup fresh basil, chopped

PREPARATION:

Cover the beans with water and soak for at least 8 hours or overnight. Drain.

In a non-stick pan, heat olive oil over medium heat. Add the onion and cook, for 3 minutes. Mix in the garlic and cook for another minute. Add the tomatoes and tomato paste, stir and cook for a few minutes. Add chicken broth, bay leaf and beans and bring to a boil, reduce the heat and simmer, uncovered, for 1 1/2 hours. Pour the bean mixture into a blender or food processor and process into a puree. Adjust the consistency with more stock if necessary. Bring large pot of salted water to boil. Cook tortellini according to package directions. Pour sauce over tortellini garnish with basil and serve.

SERVINGS: 4

Tuna Cakes and Smashed Potatoes

Ingredients:

FOR SMASHED POTATOES:

- 2 large potatoes, unpeeled, chopped
- 2 tsp salt
- 1/2 cup low fat milk
- 3 tablespoons unsalted butter

For Tuna Cakes:

- 3 tbs canola oil
- 2 (6 oz) cans tuna fish, drained
- 1 egg, beaten
- 2 tablespoons diced green onions
- 1/4 cup mayonnaise, non-fat
- 1/2 cup whole wheat bread, cut into small pieces
- Lemon juice, optional

PREPARATION:

Cook potatoes in a small saucepan until tender. Drain. Place potatoes back in pan. Heat the milk and butter in microwave until hot. With a potato masher, roughly smash the potatoes while adding hot liquid until combined and set aside. In a bowl, combine tuna, egg, green onions, mayonnaise, bread crumbs, and lemon juice. Form into patties. Allow to refrigerate and become firm for 10 minutes. Heat oil over medium-high heat, cook patties until golden brown, about 2 minutes on each side. Serve with potatoes.

SERVINGS: 4

Turkey and Barley Casserole

Ingredients:

- 3/4 lb ground turkey (or chicken)
- 1/2 tsp salt
- 1 onion, chopped finely
- 2 carrots, chopped
- 2 stalks celery, chopped
- 1 green bell pepper, seeded and chopped
- 12 button mushrooms, quartered
- 2 1/2 cups chicken stock
- 1 cup barley
- 1 tsp poultry seasoning
- 1 bay leaf

PREPARATION:

Preheat oven to 375F degrees.

In a large pan, over medium- high heat, cook ground turkey with salt until browned, about 5 minutes. Add onions, carrots, celery and green peppers. Cook until tender, about 5 minutes. Add mushrooms, stock, barley, poultry seasoning and bay leaf. Mix together and place mixture in a 9x13 inch baking dish. Cover and bake in the preheated oven for 1 hour. Serve.

SERVINGS: 4

Vegetable and Butter Bean Curry

Ingredients:

- 1 1/2 lbs butternut squash, seeded and chopped
- 1 tbs olive oil
- 1 small onion, finely sliced
- 1 tbs curry powder, mild
- 1 2/3 cups coconut milk
- 1 cup water
- 3 cups fresh spinach, chopped
- 1 (14 oz) can butter beans, drained and rinsed
- 2 tbs fresh cilantro, chopped

PREPARATION:

In a small saucepan, place squash and cover with water. Boil squash until tender and drain. In a large pan, heat olive oil and cook onions until tender. Stir in curry powder, continue stirring until fragrant, about 3 minutes. Stir in coconut milk and water.

Bring to boil; simmer, uncovered, about five minutes or until the mixture just thickens. Add squash, spinach, butter beans and cilantro. Stir until heated through. Serve.

SERVINGS: 4

Vegetable and Garbanzo Curry

Ingredients:

- 2 tablespoons vegetable oil
- 1 onion, sliced
- 2 tbs curry powder, mild
- 1/2 tsp garlic powder
- 1/4 tsp ginger, grated
- 1 (15 oz) can tomatoes, seeded and diced
- 2 (15 oz) cans garbanzo beans (do not drain)
- 2 cups potatoes, unpeeled, diced
- 1 cup sliced carrots
- 1 (16 oz) package frozen cauliflower pieces
- 1 (10 oz) package frozen peas
- Water as necessary
- 1/4 tsp salt
- 2 cups cooked, hot brown rice

PREPARATION:

In a large non-stick pan, heat oil over medium-high heat. Cook onions until softened. Add curry powder, garlic powder and ginger; cook 2 minutes. Add tomatoes, garbanzo beans, potatoes, and carrots and stir together. Add cauliflower, cover and reduce heat to simmer. Cook for 20-30 minutes, until vegetable are tender, adding water if necessary. Stir in peas and salt; cook 5 more minutes. Serve over hot rice.

SERVINGS: 4

Vegetarian Penne Pasta

Ingredients:

- 1/2 lb whole wheat penne or bowtie pasta
- 1 tbs salt
- 2 tbs extra virgin olive oil
- 8 oz sliced white mushrooms
- 8 oz asparagus, fresh, chopped (or frozen and thawed)
- 8 oz red bell pepper, seeded and chopped
- 1/4 cup Parmesan cheese, grated
- 1/4 cup fresh basil, chopped

PREPARATION:

Bring a large pot of salted water to boil. Add pasta and cook according to package directions until al dente.

While the pasta is cooking, in a medium pan, heat olive oil over medium heat. Add the mushrooms and cook for about five minutes to release all the water. Add the asparagus and bell pepper and sauté for 3-4 minutes, until softened. Add cooked pasta to pan and add Parmesan cheese, stir until well combined. Transfer to a serving bowl, garnish with fresh basil and serve.

SERVINGS: 2

SOUP RECIPES

Asparagus Soup

Ingredients:

- 1 tbs olive oil
- 1 cup shallots, chopped finely
- 3 garlic cloves, minced
- 2 lbs. asparagus, fresh (or frozen and thawed), chopped into
- one inch pieces.
- 6 cups vegetable stock, store bought or homemade
- 1 tsp salt

PREPARATION:

Reserve asparagus tops for later use. In a large soup pot, heat olive oil over medium heat. Cook shallots and garlic until softened, about 3-5 minutes. Add asparagus stalks, vegetable stock and salt and bring to a boil. Cover and reduce heat to low and simmer until asparagus softens. Let soup cool and puree with a hand blender, until creamy. Add asparagus tops and cook on medium for 5 minutes, until tops are tender.

. . .

SERVINGS: 4

Beans with Greens Soup

✦

Ingredients:

- 2 tbsp extra virgin olive oil
- 1 onion, chopped finely
- 4 garlic cloves, chopped finely
- 2 celery stalks, sliced finely
- 2 carrots, sliced finely
- 6 cups water (or chicken broth)
- 1/4 tsp thyme
- 1/4 tsp rosemary
- 1 bay leaf
- 1 (14 oz) can cannellini beans
- 1/2 tsp salt
- 1 cup leafy greens (baby spinach, chard or kale), chopped

PREPARATION:

In a large soup pot, heat olive oil over medium heat. Add onions and cook until softened, about 3 minutes. Stir in garlic, celery, and carrots and continue to cook for 5 minutes, stirring occasionally. Add water or chicken broth, thyme, rosemary and bay leaf and cook until it comes to a boil. Reduce heat and cover and simmer gently for about 45-60 minutes.

Add beans and season with salt. Let soup cool slightly, remove bay leaf and puree with a hand blender, until creamy. Add leafy greens and cook until tender, approximately 5-10 minutes, depending on the greens being used. Serve in warmed soup bowls.

SERVINGS: 4

Beef & Vegetable Soup

Ingredients:

- 1/2 lb ground beef (or turkey), lean
- 1/2 bag frozen mixed vegetables (carrot cubes, green beans, peas and broccoli)
- 1/4 cup barley
- 1 can (32 oz) beef broth, store bought or homemade
- 2 medium tomatoes, seeded, and roughly chopped
- 1 tsp garlic powder
- 1 tsp paprika
- 1 tsp oregano
- 1 bay leaf

PREPARATION:

In a large soup pot, over medium-high heat, brown ground beef. Add frozen vegetables, barley, broth, tomatoes, garlic powder, paprika, oregano and bay leaf. Bring pot to a boil, Reduce heat, cover and simmer for 30 minutes.

BARBARA CAMERON

. . .

Servings: 4

Cannellini and Butter Bean Soup

Ingredients:

- 1 tbs olive oil
- 3 strips pancetta, chopped
- 3 cloves garlic, chopped
- 2 medium red onions, finely chopped
- 2 (14 oz) cans cannellini beans, drained and rinsed
- 2 (14 oz) cans butter beans, drained and rinsed
- 2 tsp fresh thyme, chopped finely
- 1 tbs balsamic vinegar
- 6 cups vegetable stock, store bought or homemade

PREPARATION:

In a large soup pot, heat olive oil over medium-high heat. Cook pancetta until crisp. Add garlic and onions. Cook until onions are tender, about 5 minutes. Stir in beans, thyme, vinegar and vegetable stock. Bring pot to a boil, reduce heat and simmer uncovered for 15 minutes. Serve.

. . .

SERVINGS: 6

Chicken and Split Pea Soup

Ingredients:

- 1 lb. skinless, boneless chicken breast, cubed
- 2 tbs olive oil
- 2 large onions, chopped
- 3 garlic cloves, minced
- 3 carrots, grated
- 1 bay leaf
- 1 tsp salt
- 1 tsp poultry seasoning
- 8 cups chicken broth, store bought or homemade
- 1/2 cup dried split peas, washed and drained
- 1 cup green peas, fresh (or frozen and thawed)

PREPARATION:

In a large soup pot, heat olive oil over medium heat. Add chicken and cook for 5 minutes, until lightly browned. Add onions, garlic, carrots, bay leaf, salt and seasoning and cook until vegetables soften, stirring occasionally. Add broth and split peas to pot and bring to a boil. Reduce heat, cover and simmer on low heat for 30-45 minutes. To the soup, add green peas and heat for 5 minutes, stirring to combine all ingredients.

SERVINGS: 4-6

Creamy Chickpea soup

Ingredients:

- 2 1/2 cups vegetable broth, store bought or homemade
- 2 cups fresh baby spinach
- 2 cups tomatoes, seeded and chopped
- 2 cups hummus, store bought or homemade
- 1 tbs lemon juice

PREPARATION:

In a medium pot, bring vegetable broth to a boil. Add spinach and tomatoes and cook until spinach wilts, about 4 – 5 minutes. Lower heat and stir in the hummus and lemon juice and cook until heated through.

SERVINGS: 4

Creamy Squash Soup

Ingredients:

- 1 acorn squash cut lengthwise, seeds removed
- 1 sweet potato, cut lengthwise
- 4 shallots cut lengthwise
- 2 tbs olive oil
- 4 garlic cloves, unpeeled
- 4 cups vegetable broth, store bought or homemade
- 1 (14 oz.) can cannellini beans
- 1/4 cup light cream
- Salt

Preparation:

Preheat oven to 375 degrees.

Brush cut sides of squash, sweet potato and shallots with oil. Place vegetables, cut side down, in a shallow roasting pan and add garlic cloves. Roast in oven until tender, about 30 – 40 minutes. Allow vegetables to cool, and scoop out flesh of squash, sweet potato. In a soup pot, place flesh of roasted vegetables, shallots and peeled garlic. Add broth and bring to a boil. Reduce heat, and simmer, covered for 30 minutes, stirring occasionally. Pour half of the beans into the soup pot and allow soup to cool. Puree soup with a hand blender, until smooth. Add other half of beans and cream. Season to taste and simmer until warmed through, about 5 minutes. Serve in warm soup bowls.

SERVINGS: 4-6

Curried Mushroom Barley Soup

Ingredients:

- 2 tbs extra virgin olive oil
- 1 cup carrots, chopped
- 1 cup onions, chopped
- 1 lb fresh white mushrooms, sliced
- 1 1/2 cups smoked ham, chopped
- 3/4 tbs curry powder, mild
- 2 (14 oz) cans chicken broth
- 1 (14 oz) can stewed tomatoes, seedless
- 1/2 cup quick cooking barley

PREPARATION:

In a large soup pot, heat olive oil over medium-high heat. Cook carrots and onion, stirring occasionally for about 5 minutes. Add mushrooms and cook, stirring frequently until mushrooms are tender, about 5 minutes. Add ham and curry powder and cook stirring constantly for 1-

2 minutes. Stir in chicken broth, tomatoes and barley. Bring pot to a boil, then reduce heat and simmer covered, until barley is tender, about 10 minutes.

SERVINGS: 4

Kidney Bean Soup

Ingredients:

- 3 slices bacon
- 2 garlic cloves, minced
- 2 shallots, chopped
- 1 carrot, chopped
- 1 (28 oz) can kidney beans, liquid reserved
- 1/2 cup quick cooking rice
- 4 cups beef broth
- 2 bay leaves
- 1/4 tsp dried basil

PREPARATION:

In a large soup pot, cook bacon over medium heat until crisp. Crumble and set aside. In the same pan with the bacon oil, cook garlic, shallots and carrots until tender, about 5 minutes. Place the beans in blender and puree until smooth. Stir into the vegetable mixture in the pan.

Add the bacon, rice, broth, bay leaves and basil. Stir soup and bring pot to a boil. Reduce heat and simmer covered, until rice is tender, 10 minutes. Serve.

SERVINGS: 4

Lentil Soup

Ingredients:

- 2 tbs olive oil
- 1 medium onion, chopped
- 2 medium carrots, chopped
- 2 stalks celery, chopped
- 3 medium new potatoes, unpeeled and cubed
- 2 bay leaves
- 2 cups lentils, uncooked and rinsed
- 1/2 tsp thyme
- 1/2 tsp oregano
- 5 cups vegetable broth, store bought or homemade
- 3 cups water

PREPARATION:

In a large soup pot, heat olive oil over medium- high heat.

Add onion, carrots, celery, and potatoes. Cook for 7 -8 minutes or until tender. Add bay leaves, lentils, thyme and oregano. Cook for a few more minutes. Add vegetable broth and water, bring to a boil. Reduce heat to low and let simmer, covered for another 45 minutes, until lentils are soft and fall apart.

SERVINGS: 6

Mushroom Barley Soup

Ingredients:

- 2 tbs olive oil
- 2 carrots, chopped
- 1 small onion, chopped
- 5 cups white mushrooms, sliced
- 1 1/2 cups smoked ham(or pancetta), diced
- 2 tsp garlic powder
- 2 (14 oz) can chicken broth, store bought or homemade
- 1 (14 oz) can stewed tomatoes, seedless
- 1/2 cup quick cooking barley

PREPARATION:

In a large soup pot, heat oil over medium-high heat. Add carrots and onion; cook, stirring occasionally until tender, about 5 minutes. Add mushrooms; cook, stirring frequently for 5 minutes. Add ham, garlic powder, chicken broth, tomatoes and barley. Bring to a boil; reduce heat and simmer covered, until barley is tender, about 10 minutes. Serve.

SERVINGS: 4

Mushroom and Ginger Soup

Ingredients:

- 2 tsp vegetable oil
- 3 garlic cloves, crushed and peeled only
- 1 tbs fresh ginger, finely shredded
- 4 oz mushrooms, sliced
- 4 cups vegetable stock, store bought or homemade
- 1 tsp light soy sauce, optional
- 4 oz bean sprouts
- 4 oz vermicelli or thin spaghetti pasta,
- 4 tbs fresh cilantro

PREPARATION:

Bring a large pot of salted water to a boil. Add pasta and cook according to package instructions until al dente. While pasta is cooking, in a large soup pot, heat oil over medium-high heat. Add garlic, ginger and mushrooms. Stir until softened, about 3-4 minutes.

Add vegetable stock and bring to boil. Add soy sauce and bean sprouts and continue to cook until tender. To serve, place cooked noodles in individual bowls and ladle soup on top. Garnish with fresh cilantro.

SERVINGS: 4

Pea and Pesto Soup

Ingredients:

- 1 cup yellow split peas, uncooked and rinsed
- 1 (14 oz) can chicken broth, store bought or homemade
- 2 1/2 cups water
- 2 tbs prepared pesto, store bought or homemade
- 1 small zucchini, seeded, sliced
- 1/2 cup green onions, chopped
- Parmesan cheese, garnish (optional)

PREPARATION:

In a large soup pot, combine split peas, broth and water and bring to a boil. Reduce heat, cover, and simmer for 20 minutes.

Stir in pesto, zucchini, and green onions; simmer for 5 to 10 more minutes. Garnish with Parmesan cheese, if desired.

. . .

SERVINGS: 2

Smooth Broccoli Soup

Ingredients:

- 2 tbs olive oil
- 1 leek, chopped
- 1 celery stalk, chopped
- 2 garlic clove, minced
- 3 small potatoes, unpeeled, chopped
- 1/2 tsp salt
- 1 bay leaf
- 3 cups vegetable broth, store bought or homemade
- 1 1/2 cup broccoli florets, fresh (or frozen and thawed)

PREPARATION:

In a large soup pan, heat oil over medium-high heat. Cook leek, celery, garlic, potatoes, salt and bay leaf until lightly browned. Add stock and bring to a boil. Reduce heat, cover and simmer 30 minutes. Add broccoli florets to pot and bring back to a boil. Reduce heat, cover, and simmer another 5 minutes or until all vegetables are tender. Remove from heat and let cool. Remove bay leaf. Puree soup with a hand blender, until smooth. Serve.

SERVINGS: 4

Split Pea Soup

Ingredients:

- 1 tbs olive oil
- 1 medium onion, chopped
- 1 stalk celery, chopped
- 1 large carrot, chopped
- 1 medium red pepper, seeded, chopped
- 1 cup yellow split peas, uncooked and rinsed
- 2 (14 oz) cans chicken broth, store bought or homemade
- 3 cups water
- 1/4 cup plain non-fat yogurt for garnish

PREPARATION:

In a large soup pot, heat olive oil over medium- high heat.

Add onion, celery, carrot, and pepper. Cook for 7 -8 minutes or until tender. Add split peas, chicken broth and water, bring to a boil.

Reduce heat to low and let simmer, covered for 45 minutes or until peas have fallen apart. Puree soup a hand blender until smooth. Garnish with a dollop of yogurt if desired. Serve.

SERVINGS: 4

SALAD RECIPES

Bean and Couscous Salad

Ingredients:

- 1 cup couscous
- 1 1/2 cups boiling water
- 1 cup sweet yellow peppers, seeded and chopped
- 2 cups cooked black beans
- 1 small onion, chopped
- 2 cups tomatoes, seeded and chopped
- 2 medium garlic cloves, minced
- 1/2 cup rice vinegar
- 1/4 cup olive oil
- 1/2 tsp salt

PREPARATION:

In a large bowl, place the couscous with boiling water. Cover and wait until couscous has absorbed all the water. Place couscous in a bowl and add the remaining ingredients. Mix well. Serve.

. . .

BARBARA CAMERON

SERVINGS: 4

Greek White Bean and Feta Salad

Ingredients:

- 2 tbs plain yogurt, low fat
- 3 tbs extra virgin olive oil
- 2 tbs fresh lemon juice
- 3/4 tsp oregano, ground
- 1 tbs fresh mint, shredded
- 2 (14 oz) cans white cannellini beans, drained and rinsed
- 1/2 cup red onions, thinly sliced
- 3 medium tomatoes, seeded and chopped
- 1/4 cup Greek olives, pitted
- 1/2 cup feta cheese, crumbled
- 2 cups spinach leaves

PREPARATION:

In large bowl, combine yogurt, olive oil, lemon juice, oregano, and mint; whisk well. Add beans, onion, tomato, olives and feta cheese;

toss lightly. Refrigerate for at least one hour. Serve on a bed of spinach.

SERVINGS: 6

Cilantro Bean Salad

Ingredients:

- 1 (14 oz) can kidney beans
- 1 (14 oz) can garbanzo beans
- 1 medium red onion, diced
- 1 small red bell pepper, seeded and chopped

DRESSING:

- 1 cup fresh cilantro
- 1/2 cup balsamic vinegar
- 1 tablespoon Dijon mustard
- 1 1/2 teaspoons cumin
- 3 cloves garlic
- 1/2 teaspoon salt
- 1 1/2 cups extra virgin olive oil
- Juice of 1/2 lemon

PREPARATION:

In a medium bowl, combine beans, onion and bell pepper and set aside.

In a food processor, blend dressing ingredients until smooth. Pour half of the dressing over bean mixture and combine. Refrigerate at least one hour.

Pour remaining dressing over salad and mix gently just before serving. Serve at room temperature.

SERVINGS: 2 – 4

Easy Grilled Steak and Mixed Greens Salad

Ingredients:

- 1 lb sirloin steak, boneless, 1/2 inch thick
- 1 cup Italian salad dressing (divided in half)
- 8 oz mixed salad greens
- 2 med tomatoes, seeded and sliced
- 1 cup white beans, cooked and drained
- 1 medium carrot, shredded
- 1 celery stalk, shredded
- 1 med summer squash, shredded

PREPARATION:

Marinade steak with1/2 cup of the dressing in a bowl and cover. Let marinate in refrigerator for 30 minutes. Grill steak over high heat for 5-10 minutes to desired doneness. Set steak aside and let rest 10 minutes. Meanwhile, toss the salad greens with tomatoes, beans, carrot, celery, squash and remaining 1/2 cup of dressing. Cut steak across the grain into thin slices. Place vegetables on serving platter. Top with steak slices, serve.

SERVINGS: 4

Fruit Salad with Avocado

Ingredients:

- 2 large avocados, pitted and diced
- 1 peach, unpeeled, pitted and diced
- 1 Gala apple, unpeeled, cored and diced
- 1 cup cantaloupe, chopped
- 1 shallot, chopped finely
- 1 English cucumber, chopped
- 1/4 cup fresh lime juice
- 1/4 cup fresh mint, chopped
- Large lettuce leaves

PREPARATION:

In a medium bowl, combine all ingredients except the lettuce leaves. Sprinkle with lime juice and mint and toss together to combine. Let salad sit at least 10-20 minutes. Serve over 2 leaves of lettuce per serving.

. . .

SERVINGS: 4

Garbanzo and Tomato Salad

Ingredients:

- 4 medium tomatoes, seeded and chopped
- 2 (14 oz) cans garbanzos, drained and rinsed
- 1/4 cup red onions, chopped finely
- 1 cup Italian parsley, chopped finely
- 2 tbs lemon Juice
- 1/4 cup extra virgin olive oil
- 1/2 tsp salt

PREPARATION:

In a large bowl, combine tomatoes, garbanzo beans, onions and fresh parsley. Set aside. In a separate small bowl whisk together lemon juice, olive oil and salt. Pour dressing over vegetables. Mix and serve.

SERVINGS: 4

Greek Lettuce Wraps

Ingredients:

- 1/4 cup mayonnaise, low fat
- 2 tsp lemon juice
- 1/2 cup white beans, canned, cooked, drained
- 1/3 cup feta cheese, crumbled
- 2 tbs pimentos, chopped
- 8 large lettuce leaves, washed and dried
- 1/2 lb cooked chicken breast strips (preferably grilled)

PREPARATION:

In a medium bowl, combine mayonnaise and lemon juice. Stir in beans, mashing slightly with fork. Add cheese and pimentos, and mix lightly. Spread lettuce leaves evenly with bean mixture.

Top with chicken; roll up. Serve.

. . .

SERVINGS: 2

Green Bean Potato Salad

Ingredients:

- 1 1/2 lbs slender green beans
- 6 small red potatoes, unpeeled, cubed
- 1 small red onion, thinly sliced lengthwise
- 1/3 cup extra virgin olive oil
- 1/4 cup red wine vinegar
- 1/4 cup rice vinegar
- 1 tbs garlic salt
- 1 tsp sugar

PREPARATION:

In a large pot of boiling water, cook green beans and potatoes about 7 minutes or until crisp-tender. Drain and place only the beans in cold water to stop cooking process. Drain and set aside. In a large salad bowl, combine beans, potatoes and onions.

For dressing, in a small bowl, whisk together olive oil, vinegars, garlic salt and sugar. Pour dressing over vegetables and toss to coat well. Refrigerate one hour prior to serving.

SERVINGS: 4 - 6

Mixed Bean Salad

Ingredients:

- 1 can (15 oz) can green beans, drained and rinsed
- 1 can (15 oz) can wax beans, drained and rinsed
- 1 can (15 oz) can kidney beans, drained and rinsed
- 1 can (15 oz) can garbanzo beans, drained and rinsed
- 1/4 cup red onion, chopped
- 1 (8 oz) jar marinated artichokes, chopped
- 1/4 cup fresh orange juice
- 1/2 cup cider vinegar
- 1/2 cup extra virgin olive oil

PREPARATION:

In a large serving bowl, combine all of the beans, onion, and artichokes. In a separate small bowl, mix together the juice and vinegar and olive oil - adjust taste with sweetener if desired. Pour dressing over bean mixture. Stir to coat. Let marinate in refrigerator for 30 minutes prior to serving.

. . .

SERVINGS: 6

Chicken Pasta Salad

Ingredients:

- 1/2 lb. whole wheat pasta (twists or bowtie)
- 1 cup cooked chicken breast, cubed
- 1 (10 oz) package frozen chopped broccoli, thawed and drained
- 1/2 cup peas, frozen and thawed
- 1/2 cup light ranch dressing
- 1 tsp Italian blend herbs (thyme, rosemary, basil)
- 1 tbs Parmesan cheese, grated

PREPARATION:

Bring a large pot of salted water to a boil. Add pasta and cook according to package instructions until al dente. Drain.

Combine cooked pasta with chicken, broccoli and peas. Set aside. In a separate bowl, blend together dressing, herbs and cheese. Pour dressing mixture into pasta and vegetable mixture. Toss well to coat, and serve.

SERVINGS: 4

Green Bean Tuna Salad

Ingredients:

- 3 lbs green beans
- 1/2 cup mayonnaise, low fat or fat free
- 1/3 cup tarragon vinegar
- 1 tsp honey Dijon mustard
- 2 small shallots, sliced thinly
- 2 (6 oz) cans tuna fish, drained
- 2 small sprigs fresh tarragon, chopped finely

PREPARATION:

In a large pot of boiling water, add green beans. Reduce heat to low, cover and simmer 5-10 minutes until beans are tender. Drain and place beans in cold water to stop cooking process. Drain and set aside. In a large bowl, combine mayonnaise, vinegar and mustard. Add green beans, shallots and tuna fish; toss to coat with dressing. Cover and refrigerate one hour prior to serving.

Garnish with fresh tarragon and serve.

SERVINGS: 4

Grilled Shrimp and Bean Salad

Ingredients:

- 1 1/2 lbs large shrimp, cleaned, de-veined and peeled
- 1/2 cup olive oil
- 2 cloves garlic, minced
- 1/2 tsp salt
- 2 shallots, minced
- 1 tbs fresh Italian parsley, chopped
- 1 1/2 tbs fresh sage leaves, chopped
- 1 tbs red wine vinegar
- 2 (14 oz) cans cannellini beans, drained and rinsed

PREPARATION:

In a shallow glass dish, combine 1/4 cup of the olive oil with the garlic and 1/4 teaspoon of the salt. Add the shrimp and mix well. Set aside. In a medium bowl, combine the shallots with the remaining 1/4 cup oil and 1/4 teaspoon salt, parsley, sage, and vinegar. Gently stir in the beans.

Grill the shrimp over medium-high heat, turning once, until just done, about 3-5 minutes. Serve the shrimp with the bean salad.

SERVINGS: 6

Light Seafood Barley Salad

Ingredients:

- 1 cup barley
- 2 cups chicken broth, store bought or homemade
- 1/2 lb shrimp, peeled, deveined and cooked
- 1/2 lb crab meat, cooked
- 1 medium green pepper, seeded and diced
- 1 tsp Dijon mustard
- 1/2 cup mayonnaise, reduced fat
- 1/2 cup fresh basil leaves, chopped

Preparation:

In a medium saucepan, bring barley and chicken broth to a boil. Reduce heat and simmer for 30 - 40 minutes, or until the barley is tender. Drain well.

In a large serving bowl, combine the barley, shrimp, crab meat, green pepper, mustard, mayonnaise and basil and chill at least 30 minutes. Garnish with fresh basil. Serve.

SERVINGS: 4

Asian Chicken Salad

Ingredients:

- 1 cup romaine lettuce, chopped
- 1 carrot, shredded
- 1 celery, sliced thinly
- 1/4 cup red pepper, seeded, sliced thinly
- 1/2 cup chicken breast, cooked, cut into strips
- 1/4 cup mangos, chopped
- 2 tbsp lime and ginger dressing, store bought

PREPARATION:

In a medium bowl, toss together all ingredients until combined. Serve alone or with whole wheat bread slices.

SERVINGS: 1

Mango Black Bean Salad

Ingredients:

- 2 (14 oz) cans black beans, drained and rinsed
- 4 medium mangoes, peeled and diced
- 1 cup fresh Italian parsley, minced
- 2 small scallions, chopped finely
- 2 medium red peppers, seeded and diced
- 2 tbs extra virgin olive oil
- 1/2 cup balsamic or wine vinegar
- 1/4 tsp salt

PREPARATION:

In a large salad bowl, combine beans with mangoes, parsley, scallions, and red bell peppers. In a separate small bowl, whisk together the oil, vinegar and salt. Pour over vegetables and mix well. Serve.

SERVINGS: 6

Mediterranean Salmon and Potato Salad

Ingredients:

- 1 lb red potatoes, unpeeled, cut into wedges
- 1/2 cup extra virgin olive oil, plus 2 tbs more
- 2 tbs balsamic vinegar
- 1 tbs fresh rosemary, minced
- 2 cups white beans, cooked, drained
- 4 salmon fillets, 4 oz each
- 2 tbs lemon juice
- 1/4 tsp salt
- 10 oz romaine lettuce, torn
- 2 cups English cucumbers, sliced (seedless)

PREPARATION:

In a medium saucepan, bring water to a boil and cook potatoes until tender, about 10 minutes. Drain and pour potatoes back into pan.

To make dressing, in a small bowl, whisk together 1/2 cup of olive oil, vinegar and rosemary. Combine potatoes and white beans with dressing. Set aside.

In a separate medium pan, heat the remaining 2 tbs of olive oil over medium-high heat. Add salmon fillets and sprinkle with lemon juice and salt. Cook about 3 - 4 minutes on each side or until fish flakes easily. To serve, place lettuce and cucumber slices on a serving platter top with potato salad and fish fillets.

SERVINGS: 4

Red Beans and Pickle Salad

Ingredients:

- 2 (14 oz) cans red beans, drained and rinsed
- 1/4 cup water chestnuts, drained and chopped
- 1 medium red onion, chopped
- 1/4 cup pickles, sliced
- 1/2 cup olive oil
- 1/4 cup balsamic vinegar
- 1/4 tsp salt

PREPARATION:

In a medium bowl, combine red beans, water chestnuts, onion, and pickles. Set aside. In a small bowl, whisk together the olive oil, vinegar and salt. Pour over bean mix and serve.

SERVINGS: 4

Shrimp, Pasta and Spinach Salad

Ingredients:

- 1/2 lb. whole-wheat pasta (shells or tubes)
- 3/4 lb medium shrimp, peeled, deveined, and cooked
- 2 cups fresh spinach
- 2 medium Roma tomatoes, seeded and chopped
- 1/2 cup light ranch salad dressing
- 4 tbs basil, chopped coarsely
- 1/4 cup parmesan cheese, grated

PREPARATION:

Bring a large pot of salted water to a boil. Cook pasta according to package instructions until al dente. Drain. While pasta is cooking, in a large bowl, combine shrimp, spinach, tomatoes, salad dressing and cooked pasta. Refrigerate for 20 minutes. Toss together with basil and cheese. Serve.

. . .

SERVINGS: 2

Spinach and Apple Salad

Ingredients:

- 1/2 lb fresh baby spinach
- 1/2 cup cabbage, thinly sliced
- 1 large pear, unpeeled, thinly sliced
- 1/4 cup green onions, chopped finely
- 1 tbs fresh basil, chopped finely
- 2 tsp balsamic vinegar
- 1/3 cup orange juice
- 1/4 cup olive oil

PREPARATION:

In a large salad bowl, combine the spinach, cabbage, and pear. To make dressing, in a small bowl, whisk together the green onions, basil, balsamic vinegar, orange juice and olive oil. Pour dressing over salad. Serve.

. . .

BARBARA CAMERON

SERVINGS: 2

Quick Spinach Salad and Black Beans

Ingredients:

- 2 cups black beans, cooked, drained, rinsed
- 1/4 cup green onions, finely chopped
- 10 oz fresh baby spinach
- 1 med red pepper, seeded and chopped
- 1 med yellow pepper, seeded and chopped
- 1/2 cup crumbled feta cheese
- 1 cup light Italian dressing

PREPARATION:

In a medium bowl, combine beans, onions, spinach, peppers and cheese. Pour dressing on top and mix together until combined. Serve.

SERVINGS: 4

Tasty Rice Salad

Ingredients:

- 1 1/2 tbs olive oil
- 2 medium green bell peppers, seeded, chopped
- 1 cup green beans, chopped
- 1 medium onion, chopped
- 2 medium carrots, diced
- 1 cup mushrooms, sliced
- 2 medium potatoes, unpeeled, cooked, cubed
- 1/2 tsp cumin
- 1/2 tsp oregano
- 1 1/2 tbs soy sauce, low sodium
- 3 cups instant brown rice (cooked, cooled)
- 1/4 cup fresh Italian parsley, chopped
- 2 tbs lemon juice

PREPARATION:

In a large non-stick pan, heat olive oil over medium-high heat.

Cook peppers, green beans, onions, and carrots for about 5 minutes. Add mushrooms and potatoes and continue cooking

2 - 3 minutes. Add cumin, oregano and soy sauce. Transfer mixture to a large salad bowl and allow to cool to room temperature. Add rice, chopped parsley and lemon juice. Mix together until combined. Serve.

SERVINGS: 6

Tuna and Bean Salad

Ingredients:

- 2 (14 oz) cans cannellini beans, drained and rinsed
- 2 (6 oz) cans tuna fish, drained
- 4 tbs extra virgin olive oil
- 2 tbs lemon juice
- 1/4 tsp salt
- 1 tbs fresh Italian parsley, minced
- 1/2 cup green onions, chopped

PREPARATION:

Place beans into serving dish. Pour the tuna evenly over the beans. In a separate, small bowl, prepare the dressing by whisking together the oil, lemon juice, salt and parsley until well combined. Pour dressing over the tuna and beans. Sprinkle onions over the bean salad and mix well. Serve.

. . .

SERVINGS: 4

Zesty Bean and Tomato Salad

Ingredients:

- 2 cans (14 oz each) white beans, drained, rinsed
- 2 cups green beans, fresh, cut in 1 inch pieces
- 2 cups tomatoes, seeded and chopped
- ¼ cup fresh Italian parsley
- 2 cups fresh arugula
- ½ cup extra virgin olive oil
- 2 tbs fresh lemon juice
- ¼ tsp salt
- 2 tbs fresh basil, chopped
- 2 tbs parmesan cheese, grated

PREPARATION:

In a medium salad bowl, combine beans, tomatoes, parsley and arugula. Set aside. To make dressing, whisk together oil, lemon juice, salt and basil until well combined. Toss vegetables with dressing and refrigerate one hour prior to serving. Top with grated cheese and serve.

. . .

SERVINGS: 4

SNACK RECIPES

Baked Sweet Potato Fries

Ingredients:

- 4 small sweet potatoes, unpeeled
- 1 tbs butter, melted
- 1/4 tsp salt
- 1 dash nutmeg

PREPARATION:

Preheat oven to 450F degrees.

Spray a large baking pan with non-stick cooking spray. Scrub potatoes and cut lengthwise into quarters, then cut each quarter into 2 wedges. Arrange potatoes in a single layer in pan. In a small bowl, combine butter, salt, and nutmeg. Brush mixture onto potatoes and coat evenly. Bake in oven 20 minutes or until brown and tender.

SERVINGS: 4

Baked Yams

Ingredients:

- 1 cup dried prunes
- 3 medium yams, unpeeled, cut into 1/4 inch squares
- 2 tsp butter, melted
- 2 tbs lemon juice
- 2 tbs fruit juice (orange or apple)
- 1/2tsp salt

PREPARATION:

Preheat oven to 350F degrees.

Soak prunes in a small bowl of warm water for 10 minutes and then drain. Steam yams over boiling water, until tender.

Spray a medium baking pan with non-stick cooking spray.

Arrange yams in a single layer in pan. Brush with butter. Top with layer of prunes. Alternate layers until all are used. In a small bowl, blend juices and salt together and pour over yams and prunes. Bake in oven for 35 minutes or until tender.

SERVINGS: 4

Citrus Carrots

Ingredients:

- 1 lb baby carrots
- 2 tbs balsamic vinegar
- 1/2 cup orange juice
- 1 large orange, peeled and chopped into small segments
- 1 tbs green onions, chopped finely
- 1 tbs fresh dill, chopped

PREPARATION:

Steam carrots in a steamer until tender or plunge carrots into boiling water and cook for about 10 - 12 minutes until tender.

Drain. Rinse with cold water and drain again.

In a medium bowl, combine carrots, vinegar and orange juice. Stir to combine. Add orange segments, onions and dill. Lightly toss and serve.

. . .

SERVINGS: 3

Honey Baked Apples

Ingredients:

- 4 medium baking apples (golden delicious), unpeeled
- 1/2 cup brown sugar
- 1/2 tsp cloves, ground
- 1/2 tsp cinnamon
- 1/2 cup honey
- 1/2 cup water

PREPARATION:

Preheat oven to 400 degrees.

Core and slice apples into 1/2" rings. Place them in a shallow baking dish for later use. In a small saucepan, combine and heat brown sugar, cloves, cinnamon, honey and water. Pour over apples and bake 15 minutes or until tender, turning to baste once or twice. Serve.

. . .

SERVINGS: 4

Kidney Bean Salsa

Ingredients:

- 1 (14 oz) red kidney beans, drained and rinsed
- 2 medium tomatoes, seeded and chopped
- 1 medium yellow pepper, seeded and chopped
- 1 medium avocado, chopped
- 1 tbs cilantro, finely chopped
- 2 tbs lime juice
- 1/4 tsp salt

PREPARATION:

In large bowl, mix all ingredients until combined well.

Serve with warm tortillas or whole wheat chips.

SERVINGS: 4

White Bean Puree

Ingredients:

- 1 (14 oz) can cannellini beans, drained and rinsed
- 2 garlic cloves
- 1/4 cup fresh Italian parsley
- Juice of 1/2 lemon
- 1/4 tsp oregano
- 1/2 tsp salt
- 1/3 cup extra virgin olive oil

PREPARATION:

Blend all ingredients in a food processor until almost smooth. Serve with crusty bread, whole wheat crackers, or fresh vegetables.

SERVINGS: 4

HOLIDAY RECIPES

Holiday Stuffing

Ingredients:

- 1 loaf of whole wheat sandwich bread, cubed
- ¾ stick of unsalted butter
- 3 large tart apples (Granny Smith), unpeeled, chopped
- 1 onion, chopped
- 3 celery stalks, chopped
- 2 cups chicken broth
- ½ cup dried apricots
- ½ cup prunes, chopped
- ½ cup Italian parsley, chopped
- ½ tbs salt

PREPARATION:

Preheat oven to 400 degrees. Lay cubed bread on a baking sheet in a single layer and bake, until toasted, about 10 minutes. Allow to cool. While bread is toasting, prepare fruit mixture. Heat butter in a large pan over medium-high heat. Add apples, onion, and celery and cook until softened, about 8-10 minutes. Put mixture in a large bowl and combine with toasted bread, broth, apricots, prunes, parsley and salt. Transfer mixture to a 3-quart baking dish and cover with foil. Bake 20 minutes, remove foil and bake an additional 15 minutes.

SERVINGS: 4

Broccoli and Potato Casserole

Ingredients:

- 6 large red potatoes, unpeeled and cubed
- 2 (10 oz) boxes chopped broccoli, defrosted
- 4 tbs butter
- 4 cloves garlic, finely chopped
- 1/2 cup cream
- ½ tbs salt
- 1/4 teaspoon freshly grated nutmeg

PREPARATION:

Place potatoes in a pot and cover with water. Add salt to water and boil potatoes until almost tender, about 6 to 8 minutes. Add broccoli and cook until tender, an additional 5-7 minutes.

Drain potatoes and broccoli. Melt butter in the hot pot, then add the garlic and cook 2 to 3 minutes. Stir in cream; add potatoes and broccoli and season with salt, pepper and nutmeg. Mash until desired consistency.

SERVINGS: 4 – 6

Easy Creamy Pumpkin Soup

Ingredients:

- 1 tablespoon extra-virgin olive oil
- 1/4 cup chopped onion
- 1 tbs curry powder
- 1 (15-ounce) can pumpkin puree
- 2 cups vegetable broth
- 2 tbs pure maple syrup
- ½ tbs salt
- 1 (14-ounce) can unsweetened coconut milk

PREPARATION:

In a large pot, heat oil over medium heat. Add the onion. Cover and cook until softened, 5 minutes. Stir in curry powder and the pumpkin puree, then whisk in the broth until smooth. Add the maple syrup and season with salt. Simmer for 10 minutes, stirring occasionally.

Using a hand-held blender, puree the soup in the pot. Otherwise, transfer the soup to a blender or food processor and puree until smooth. Stir back into the pot. Reduce heat to low. Whisk in the coconut milk, Heat until hot, but, do not boil.

SERVINGS: 4

No Bake Pumpkin Pie

Ingredients:

- 1 (9 inch) prepared graham cracker crust
- 1 (.25 ounce) package unflavored gelatin
- 1 tsp ground cinnamon
- 1/2 tsp ground nutmeg
- 1/2 tsp salt
- 1 (14 ounce) can sweetened condensed milk
- 2 eggs, beaten
- 1 (15 ounce) can pumpkin puree

PREPARATION:

In a heavy saucepan combine gelatin, cinnamon, ginger, nutmeg, and salt. Stir in condensed milk and beaten eggs, mixing well. Let stand one minute, then place on burner over low heat, stirring constantly for about 10 minutes, or until gelatin dissolves and mixture thickens. Remove from heat.

Stir in pumpkin, mixing thoroughly, and pour mixture into graham cracker crust. Chill for at least 3 hours before serving.

Beans and Tomato Salad

Ingredients:

- 2 (14 oz) cans, white beans, drained and rinsed
- 2 cups fresh green beans (cut into 1-inch pieces)
- 2 cups seedless plum tomatoes, chopped
- 1/2 cup readymade Italian dressing
- 2 tbs chopped fresh basil
- 2 tbs Parmesan cheese grated

PREPARATION:

In a medium serving bowl, combine first four ingredients together. Garnish with basil and cheese. Can be served with whole wheat pita bread triangles.

SERVINGS: 3-4

Delicious Sweet Potatoes

Ingredients:

- 4 pounds sweet potatoes, peeled and cut to large bite-sized pieces
- 2 cups orange juice
- 3 cups light corn syrup
- 1 tsp ground cinnamon
- 1 tsp ground nutmeg
- ¼ cup vanilla extract
- 2 tsp lemon zest
- 2 tbs flour
- 1 ½ cups light brown sugar, packed
- 1 ½ cups granulated sugar

PREPARATION:

Preheat oven to 350 degrees. Boil sweet potatoes until slightly underdone. Drain, cool and set aside. In a large bowl, whisk together orange juice, corn syrup, cinnamon, nutmeg, vanilla and zest. In another bowl, combine flour and both sugars together. Put cooled sweet potatoes in a deep baking dish, add dry ingredient mixture and stir to coat. Pour liquid over yams and bake for 20 to 25 minutes.

SERVINGS: 6-8

Turkey Cutlets with Sage

Ingredients:

- 4 tsp red wine vinegar
- 2 tsp minced garlic
- 2 tsp dried sage leaves
- 1 pound turkey breast cutlets
- Salt and pepper, to taste
- 1/4 cup whole wheat flour
- 2 tsp olive oil
- 1/2 cup reduced-sodium fat-free chicken broth
- 1 tbs lemon juice

PREPARATION:

Lay a large sheet of plastic wrap on the counter; sprinkle with half the combine vinegar, garlic, and sage. Place cutlets on plastic wrap; sprinkle with remaining vinegar mixture. Sprinkle lightly with salt and pepper. Cover cutlets with second sheet of plastic wrap. Using kitchen mallet or bottom of heavy pan, pound cutlets to flatten. Let stand 5 minutes.

Sprinkle both sides of cutlets with flour. Heat oil in large skillet over medium-high heat; add half the cutlets and cook until browned on bottom, about 1-1/2 minutes. Turn and cook on second side until cooked through, about 3 minutes. Remove cutlets to oven-proof serving platter; keep warm. Repeat with remaining cutlets.

Heat broth and lemon juice to boiling in skillet; cook until reduced by half. Pour mixture over cutlets; serve immediately.

SERVINGS: 4

Spinach and Mushroom Toss

Ingredients:

- 2 teaspoons olive oil
- 1/4 cup shallots, minced
- 3 cloves garlic, minced
- 3 strips turkey bacon, chopped
- 4 cups of white mushrooms, sliced
- 3 tbs balsamic vinegar
- 1 1/2 tbs reduced-sodium soy sauce
- 2 (10oz) bags fresh baby spinach

PREPARATION:

In a large pan, heat olive oil over medium heat. Add shallots and garlic and cook for 1 minute. Add turkey bacon and cook an additional 2-3 minutes, or until browned. Add mushrooms and cook 3 to 5 minutes, until mushrooms are tender. Add balsamic vinegar and soy sauce and bring to a simmer. Add spinach and simmer 1 to 2 minutes, until spinach wilts, turning frequently.

. . .

SERVINGS: 4-5